Represe̶n̶t̶i̶n̶g Religions

Teachers of RE from six religions
explain how to share
their religions in the classroom

A PCfRE project generously supported by
the St Luke's College Trust and the Spalding Trust

Edited by Lat Blaylock, with an introductory chapter by
Professor Robert Jackson, University of Warwick

RE Today Services, a part of Christian Education, is an ecumenical educational charity which works throughout the United Kingdom. Its aims are:

- to support Religious Education in schools;
- to increase awareness of the spiritual, moral, social and cultural dimensions of the curriculum;
- to articulate Christian perspectives on education.

RE Today Services is committed to the teaching of the major world faiths in Religious Education, and to an accurate and fair representation of their beliefs, values and practices in all its teaching materials.

RE Today Services fulfils these aims:

- by publishing teaching materials and background papers together with a termly magazine *REtoday*, and distributing the *British Journal of Religious Education*;
- by offering professional development and consultancy services through its professional staff;
- by arranging national and regional courses for teachers, pupils and others interested in education;
- by research and curriculum development work;
- by supporting the Professional Council for Religious Education and distributing its journal *Resource*.

The Professional Council for Religious Education is the subject teacher association for RE professionals in primary and secondary schools and higher education, providing a focal point for their concerns, a representative voice at a national level, and publications and courses to enable professional development.

PCfRE works through its Executive and Executive Officer to address the real concerns of all RE teachers by:

- publishing the journal *Resource*;
- running courses for RE teachers;
- offering support to local RE teachers' groups;
- monitoring government action and inaction with regard to RE, and responding to consultation documents;
- pressing the case for more time, staff, training and money for RE.

PCfRE members number around 2,500 including students, primary RE co-ordinators, and subject specialists in secondary schools. They receive *REtoday* and *Resource* each term, and are entitled to discounts on courses and RE Today Services publications. They may nominate members of the Executive or stand for office themselves. We hope members value all of these opportunities. We know that we need all RE professionals to join us.

Edited by Lat Blaylock

Published by Christian Education Publications
1020 Bristol Road
Selly Oak
Birmingham
B29 6LB

British Cataloguing-in-Publication data
A catalogue record for this book is available from the British Library

ISBN 1-904024-06-8

First published 2004

Designed and typeset by Christian Education Publications

Printed and bound by Martins the Printers Ltd, Berwick upon Tweed

Preface

This book from the Professional Council for Religious Education is a sign of the pluralising professionalism of the RE teachers of the United Kingdom.

In the six chapters written by practising members of the UK's major faith communities, any teacher of RE will find stimulus, provocation and guidance about the ways in which different religions are represented in the curriculum – any teacher using the unique insights collected here will be able to develop better RE practice. The voices you will hear through these pages are authentic RE voices – our contributors know the demands of the classroom, and the challenge that restive children and young people offer to learning about religions. They are also authentic because they come from those who practice the faith – never in an all-encompassing way, but always with some integrity and insight. This is a rare combination of two authenticities, and we are delighted to present these 'voices' to all RE professionals.

PCfRE initiated the project that has led to this publication with two generous grants from the St Luke's College Foundation and the Spalding Trust. We record here our gratitude to these trusts for their support in bringing together the teams and groups that have created these pages.

Our intention in this work has not been to provide academically oriented studies of the six religions – many such exist already. Instead, we have taken the view that anyone who is a faith insider but also a classroom insider will have some insights into how to teach their faith. So a diversity of belief and practice among our sixteen contributors is unified by the shared experience: we are all RE teachers.

Whether you are a new teacher, or have decades of experience, we hope these articles will give you food for thought, insight to chew over and the appetite to do RE even better.

Lat Blaylock
PCfRE Executive Officer

Contents

Introduction:
Representing and interpreting religions

Professor Robert Jackson

Professor Robert Jackson leads the University of Warwick's Religions and Education Research Unit. He is the editor of the British Journal of Religious Education, and was the key speaker at PCfRE's 'Representing Religions' conference for teachers of RE from six faiths. This introductory chapter addresses some of the difficult questions about how religions can be represented in the classroom: who speaks for the faith? Can children and young people really understand the life world of a religion they don't belong to? In what ways do current approaches distort religions? Can these distortions teach us a better way? In addressing these complex questions, Robert Jackson provides an academic base for reflection upon the 'insiders' articles, written by RE teachers from six different religions, which follow.

Since interpretation involves the learner in comparing currently understood concepts and past experiences with those of others, the student's own perspective is an essential part of the learning process.

In *Religious Education: An Interpretive Approach*, I argued that if Religious Education includes at least understanding the religious worldviews of others, then a range of issues about the representation of religious material and methods for interpreting it need to be addressed (Jackson 1997). In particular, I pointed to the dangers of representing religious worldviews as bounded systems of belief and proposed a more personal and flexible model allowing for the uniqueness of each person, while giving due attention to the various influences which help to shape any individual's sense of personal and social identity.

I also developed some methods for interpreting religious material, especially drawing on insights from various strands of social anthropology. Rather than expecting students to set aside their own presuppositions when studying other positions (as usually required in phenomenological approaches), these methods made direct use of their concepts and past experiences. Since interpretation involves the learner in comparing currently understood concepts and past experiences with those of others, the student's own perspective is an essential part of the learning process. This matter is very important from the point of view of teaching, since educators need to be sensitive to students' own positions in devising strategies for teaching and learning about the worldviews of others.

Finally I also discussed various elements of reflexivity, broadly understood to refer to different aspects of the relationship between the experience of students (or researchers) and the experience of those whose way of life they are attempting to interpret. I have drawn attention to three aspects of reflexivity:

- the learner re-assessing her or his understanding of her or his own way of life (being 'edified' through reflecting on another's way of life);
- making a constructive critique of the material studied at a distance;
- developing a running critique of the interpretive process – being methodologically self-critical (Jackson 2000).

These points too have implications for pedagogy. There needs to be an approach to teaching that encourages reflection and constructive criticism. The more the teacher is aware of the religious and ideological backgrounds of students, the more sensitive and focused the teaching can be, whether it be through discussion or the setting of activities. The pedagogy for this approach to RE also requires methods that allow students to gain insight from their peers and to be able to examine different ideas of truth held within the classroom. The 'content' of RE is not simply data provided by

the teacher, but includes the knowledge and experience of the participants and an interactive relationship between the two. The specialist Religious Education teacher, working with children from diverse backgrounds, needs the professional skill to manage learning that is dialectical. If teachers can have the right degree of sensitivity towards their students' own positions, as well as to the material studied, and can develop appropriate pedagogies, then a genuinely conversational form of RE can take place which can handle diversity.

'Insiders' and 'outsiders'

The issues of representation, interpretation and reflexivity are closely related. Edward Said's seminal work on *Orientalism* (1978), for example, provides a historical dimension, showing how aspects of Islam were constructed and represented stereotypically by Europeans in their own interests. For Said, Orientalist interpretations have more to do with self-definition through giving stereotyped portraits of the 'other' than with providing reliable and self-critical accounts of another's way of life. A major fault with such interpretations was their lack of self-criticism, leading to an institutionalised view of knowledge, perpetuated inter-textually.

Clearly, one's position on interpretation depends on where one stands in relation to the debate about the relationship between insiders and outsiders in the study of religions and cultures. At one extreme, there are those who see religions and cultures as 'closed', changing over time, but maintaining a bedrock of core values and beliefs, and having distinct boundaries (for example McIntyre 1978). Here the distinction between insider and outsider is clear and sharp. At the other extreme, there are those who would make a case for the complete deconstruction of religion(s) and cultures. The focus is solely on individuals and their personal narratives. Clive and Jane Erricker's anti-realist postmodern position on Religious Education is a case in point. They argue, for example, that any pre-prepared materials for pupils impose particular constructions of reality on children and should be avoided (Erricker and Erricker 2000).

In the case of both 'religions' and 'cultures' I would argue for a middle way. The European Enlightenment view of 'religions' as discrete belief systems should be abandoned in favour of a much looser portrayal of religious traditions and groupings, variously delimited and politically contested by different practitioners and non-practitioners, and in which some individuals may locate themselves or be located by others. Individuals they are, but they need to be seen in relation to a range of contextual group influences, some of which may be outside the religious tradition (Jackson 1997, Chapter 3).

Similarly, individuals might be seen as part of a cultural tradition, in the sense that they maintain or modify certain practices (perhaps in a climate of contest or conflict); however, they also may draw on a range of cultural resources available to them from a variety of locations. This is especially so if they live in plural and globalised societies where they may experience complex interactions and mutual influences with others, as well as being open to influence from the media and the internet. With this position, no single metaphor is capable of capturing the complexity of cultural experience. The categories of 'insider' and 'outsider' are hard to apply with consistency. There may be some areas where religious and/or cultural experience overlaps and thus is shared, but others where a distinction between insider and outsider is clearer. Moreover, social context determines to some extent which elements of a person's identity are in the foreground.

In late modern pluralistic societies, individuals might identify with aspects of a cultural tradition, argue with other aspects and also draw creatively on new resources in reshaping their own cultural identities. As Gerd Baumann has demonstrated, much cultural reshaping and creativity takes place when people of different backgrounds

The European Enlightenment view of 'religions' as discrete belief systems should be abandoned in favour of a much looser portrayal of religious traditions and groupings, variously delimited and politically contested by different practitioners and non-practitioners, and in which some individuals may locate themselves or be located by others.

interact at sites of mutual or overlapping interest (Baumann 1996). As well as seeing a person as part of a continuing, yet contested, cultural tradition (Clifford 1986, Said 1978), it is *also* possible to observe that person drawing on and being creative with new cultural material. What are of particular interest are the *processes* of cultural change, and the influence of context on cultural expression.

> **What are of particular interest are the processes of cultural change, and the influence of context on cultural expression.**

To make this outline of a middle position more concrete, Eleanor Nesbitt's longitudinal study of young British Hindus reveals some very different individuals having a sense of 'being Hindu' as an important part of their personal and social identity, and yet drawing eclectically (and in their own different ways) on religio-cultural material outside as well as within Hindu tradition (for example Nesbitt 1998, 2000). One young woman, 'Mina', interviewed at ages 12 (when a school girl) and 21 (when a psychology student), drew on her family and personal experience as a devotee of Sathya Sai Baba as well as on sources such as Western music in developing her own exploratory spirituality. This young woman, at 21, still connected with her experience of Hindu bhakti tradition, especially through meditative practice. She also maintained a strong social concern, consistent with Sathya Sai Baba's teaching. However, she has abandoned ritual practices that she followed as a 12-year-old in the context of family life, preferring the expression of a theistic spirituality rather than what she regards as the practice of a religion.

The identities of Nesbitt's interviewees emerge as plural, complex and integrated. They relate to each other through a common sense of connectedness with Hindu tradition (and thereby display a family resemblance); however, in some ways, the young people are very different from each other. Interestingly, Nesbitt's own experience as a member of the Society of Friends, with a strong interest in the spiritual quest, especially 'overlapped' at some points with that of 'Mina', facilitating the interpretive process. The encounter affected both of them (Nesbitt 2001).

So far I have pointed to the dangers of reifying religions and cultures, yet defending the usage of the terms with certain caveats and in particular contexts. I have also pleaded for a high degree of flexibility in portraying the individual as part of religious or cultural space, and for using a range of metaphors to portray religious or cultural identity. I have further presented both qualitative research and classroom learning as circular, interpretive processes, involving comparison and contrast of concepts and experiences, personal reflection and self-criticism with regard to method.

Experimental curriculum development

Many of the above points were used in a curriculum development project, the Warwick RE Project (WREP), in which a team of writers and researchers attempted to apply them in the production of texts for use by children aged 5–13 (Barratt 1994a, b, c, d, e; Barratt and Price 1996a and b; Everington 1996a and b; Jackson, Barratt and Everington 1994; Mercier 1996; Robson 1995; Wayne et al 1996). In designing experimental curriculum materials to help teachers and pupils to use this approach, the WREP team drew on ethnographic research on children related to different religious communities and groups in Britain, and on theory from the social sciences, literary criticism, religious studies and other sources (Jackson 1997, Chapter 5). The intention was to provide a methodology that was epistemologically open and genuinely conversational. The framework for teaching and learning encouraged sensitive and skilful interpretation, opportunities for constructive criticism (including pupils' reflections on their own use of interpretive methods), and reflection by students on what they had studied. However, we do not suggest that the particular way we approached pedagogy was the only possible one, nor that the source material for interpretive approaches should always be ethnographic. Ethnographic reports generally do, however, move straight to individual cases and bring a humanising element to the study of religion.

Wider applications of an interpretive approach

Whereas the pedagogy of the Warwick RE Project started from a consideration of the young people portrayed in the curriculum texts, the interpretive approach considered more generally can start at any point on the hermeneutic circle. The approach could start with an overview of a tradition, followed by a consideration of specific examples. This is what Dermot Killingley and I did in writing an introductory text for students and teachers entitled *Approaches to Hinduism* (Jackson and Killingley 1988). The book starts with an overview of the Hindu tradition, but its limitations are pointed out to readers. There follows a treatment of some specific elements from the tradition through a series of case studies of individual Hindus. The source material for these was either ethnographic or biographical. The intention was that the introduction should make the case studies intelligible, while the case studies provided details of religious life, some of which were not generalisable, to point up the limitations of the overview and to extend an understanding of the Hindu tradition. Denise Cush has taken an analogous approach in introducing the Jain tradition through some of its key ideas, and taking care to include the experience of the learner as part of the hermeneutic circle (Cush 1999).

Representations by 'insiders'

Writers and curriculum developers who identify with a particular religious tradition have a special responsibility in representing religions. On the one hand, they have the advantage of the personal knowledge and experience of the insider. On the other hand, they may find it difficult to present a balanced overview of the wider tradition, or feel impelled to present a view of orthodoxy that is inconsistent with the experience of many practitioners. Possible approaches include:

- providing a personal story of their own religious and cultural experience, with some pointers to further examples of the wider tradition;

- working with others from the same tradition, not to attempt to find essential common ground (as with the School Curriculum and Assessment Authority's Model Syllabuses for RE, produced by faith community working groups in 1994), but to give some different perspectives on how the tradition is lived in practice.

Insiders who are also teachers (whether acting in the role of teacher or writer) are especially in a position to help children from other backgrounds to make connections, comparisons and contrasts between the children's own knowledge and experience and their own.

> Insiders who are also teachers (whether acting in the role of teacher or writer) are especially in a position to help children from other backgrounds to make connections, comparisons and contrasts between the children's own knowledge and experience and their own.

References

Barratt, M (1994a), *An Egg for Babcha*, *Bridges to Religions* series, The Warwick RE Project, Oxford, Heinemann.

Barratt, M (1994b), *Lucy's Sunday*, *Bridges to Religions* series, The Warwick RE Project, Oxford, Heinemann.

Barratt, M (1994c), *Something to Share*, *Bridges to Religions* series, The Warwick RE Project, Oxford, Heinemann.

Barratt, M (1994d), *The Buddha's Birthday*, *Bridges to Religions* series, The Warwick RE Project, Oxford, Heinemann.

Barratt, M (1994e), *The Seventh Day is Shabbat*, *Bridges to Religions* series, The Warwick RE Project, Oxford, Heinemann.

Barratt, M and Price, J (1996a), *Meeting Christians: Book One*, *Bridges to Religions* series, The Warwick RE Project, Oxford, Heinemann.

Barratt, M and Price, J (1996b), *Teacher's Resource Book: Meeting Christians: Book One*, *Bridges to Religions* series, The Warwick RE Project, Oxford, Heinemann.

Baumann, G (1996) *Contesting Culture: Discourses of Identity in Multi-Ethnic London*, Cambridge, Cambridge University Press.

Clifford, James (1986), 'Introduction: Partial Truths' in J Clifford and G Marcus (eds), *Writing Culture: The Poetics and Politics of Ethnography*, Berkeley, University of California Press, 1–26.

Cush, Denise (1999) 'Learning From the Concept and Concepts of a Religious Tradition, *Journal of Beliefs and Values*, 20 (1), 60–74.

Erricker, C and Erricker, J (2000), *Reconstructing Religious, Spiritual and Moral Education,* London, Routledge/Falmer.

Everington, J (1996a), *Meeting Christians: Book Two, Bridges to Religions* series, The Warwick RE Project, Oxford, Heinemann.

Everington, J (1996b), *Teacher's Resource Book: Meeting Christians: Book Two, Bridges to Religions* series, The Warwick RE Project, Oxford, Heinemann.

Ipgrave, J (2001), *Pupil-to-Pupil Dialogue in the Classroom as a Tool for Religious Education*, Warwick Religions and Education Research Unit, Working Paper 2, Coventry, Institute of Education, University of Warwick.*

Jackson, R (1997), *Religious Education: An Interpretive Approach*, London, Hodder and Stoughton.

Jackson, R (2000), 'The Warwick Religious Education Project: The Interpretive Approach to Religious Education', in M H Grimmitt (ed), *Pedagogies of Religious Education: Case Studies in the Research and Development of Good Pedagogic Practice in RE*, Great Wakering, McCrimmons, 130–52.

Jackson, R, Barratt, M and Everington, J (1994), *Bridges to Religions: Teacher's Resource Book*, The Warwick RE Project, Oxford, Heinemann.

Jackson, R and Killingley, D (1988), *Approaches to Hinduism*, London, John Murray.

Mcintyre, J (1978), *Multi-Culture and Multifaith Societies: Some Examinable Assumptions*, Occasional Papers, Oxford, Farmington Institute for Christian Studies.

Mercier, Carrie (1996), *Muslims, Interpreting Religions* series, The Warwick RE Project, Oxford, Heinemann.

Nesbitt, E (1998), 'British, Asian and Hindu: Identity, Self-narration and the Ethnographic Interview', *Journal of Beliefs and Values*, 19 (2), 189–200.

Nesbitt, E (2001), 'Religious Nurture and Young People's Spirituality: Reflections on Research at the University of Warwick' in Jane Erricker, Cathy Ota and Clive Erricker (eds), *Spiritual Education: Cultural, Religious and Social Differences: New Perspectives for the 21st Century*, Brighton, Sussex Academic, 130–42.

Østberg, S (1999), *Pakistani Children in Oslo: Islamic Nurture in a Secular Setting*, Unpublished PhD Thesis, Institute of Education, University of Warwick. (This thesis will be published shortly by the Community Religions Project, University of Leeds, UK).

Robson, G (1995), *Christians, Interpreting Religions* series, The Warwick RE Project, Oxford, Heinemann.

Said, E (1978), *Orientalism*, London, Routledge and Kegan Paul.

Wayne, E, Everington, J, Kadodwala, D and Nesbitt, E (1996), *Hindus, Interpreting Religions* series, The Warwick RE Project, Oxford, Heinemann.

---

* See also Østberg (1999) for discussion of the concept of integrated plural identity in relation to her Pakistani interviewees in Oslo.

Helping teachers tackle my religion in the classroom
Guidance from inside the Buddhist faith

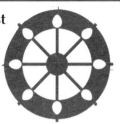

The four contributors to this section come from disparate points within the Buddhist traditions. The first section of the article is the product of co-operation between Adiccabandhu and Liz Andrews. Then two perspectives, from Robin Jackson and from Gary Beesley, provide additional sources for teachers. All four of our Buddhist contributors are teachers of RE. Their material is supplemented with quotations from other sources.

Buddhism among the religions

Adiccabandhu and Liz Andrews explore Buddhism's relations with other religions, and some common questions asked about Buddhism in schools.

The first and highest ethical principle of Buddhism is that of non-harm, or nonviolence. Buddhism teaches that it is never justified to harm another on the basis of belief. This principle is tested in situations where people hold conflicting beliefs. The appropriate response in such situations is tolerance. Tolerance is the first principle of non-harm applied to conflict situations. Tolerance does not mean that we all have to agree on what we believe – that would be a sort of universalism, a belief that all religions are essentially the same (an argument which Buddhists refute).

Tolerance means that all people are free to practise and propagate their beliefs. In such a society, there can be full and frank exchange of critiques of other religions – free of charges of blasphemy, for example.

The Buddha advised his followers that the appropriate response to criticism of Buddhism is not anger, but to calmly examine the criticism being made. If it is untrue, then point out the error' if true, acknowledge it and take action to correct oneself. History shows that on some occasions, some Buddhist sects, in their encounters with each other, have fallen short of the practice of their own highest moral principle, nonviolence, and those Buddhists stand criticised for that.

The Buddhist Emperor Ashoka, who ruled a large part of India about 150 BCE, decreed that people of all religions should reside peacefully together in his empire. That is the ideal we should all aspire to.

> For hatred can never put an end to hatred; love alone can. This is an unalterable law.
> *Dhammapada 1:5*

Presenting Buddhism in schools – some common questions pupils ask

Do Buddhists believe in God?

No, Buddhists do not believe in a creator God who made all things, and who will judge them in the hereafter. It is axiomatic to Buddhism that people are responsible for, and have ultimate control of their own destiny (the law of karma). Buddhists also believe that there is no upper limit to their potential. All have the potential for the unlimited state of Enlightenment. The Buddhist scriptures give an account of an encounter between the Buddha and a god who claimed to be the eternal creator God. The Buddha refuted his assertion (Majjhima-Nikaya Sutta 49).

If the Buddha is not God, why do Buddhists worship him?

The word 'worship' has a wider connotation in the East than in the West. In the East, worship means to pay respect or homage, or show appreciation, 'worth-ship'. One

> All the effort must be made by you; Buddhas only show the way. Follow this path and practise meditation.
> *Dhammapada 20:276*

can even worship one's teacher! For Westerners, the word worship tends to mean the veneration paid only to God.

Buddhists worship the Buddha for several reasons. They worship in order to express their gratitude for his teaching. They will also worship in order to strengthen their own desire to strive for Enlightenment. In a way they are paying homage to the potential for Enlightenment latent within all beings.

Many Buddhists also believe that the Buddha is present to them, and can support and inspire them in their quest.

Who is the Buddha?

For Buddhists, the Buddha was a human being who went beyond the limitations of the human state by gaining the unlimited state of Enlightenment. There are gods, or divine beings, in Buddhism, but they too are subject to impermanence, and are therefore not eternal. Enlightenment is beyond any limited state, human or divine.

Is the Dalai Lama the world leader of Buddhism?

No. There is no central authority in Buddhism. From the beginning, Buddhism has had its diversity. The Buddha did not require obedience on his own behalf, or on the behalf of a creator God. The different schools of Buddhism have evolved around variety of practice rather than variety of belief.

The Dalai Lama is head of one of the Tibetan schools of Buddhism, and spiritual leader of the Tibetan people. He is admired and respected by all Buddhists as a shining example of the principle of nonviolence in the face of Chinese oppression of Buddhism in Tibet.

If they have no God to judge them why do Buddhists practise morality?

The law of karma states that moral action leads to happiness, while immoral action leads to unhappiness. This law of karma is a law of the universe, not a divine law. Moral actions spring from motivations of generosity, love and wisdom, while immoral actions express the opposite: greed, hatred and ignorance. On the basis of a sound ethical character built on ethics, Buddhism says that one can meditate effectively, and so gain Enlightenment.

Adiccabandhu

Adiccabandhu is a member of the Western Buddhist Order, which was founded by Sangharakshita in 1968. Adiccabandhu is a practising primary school teacher of many years' experience, and an RE co-ordinator. He has written materials on Buddhism for all the key stages for The Clear Vision Trust, and has given initial teacher training and in-service training on the teaching of Buddhism. He has also written several children's books on Buddhism.

Liz Andrews

Liz Andrews is a Buddhist and an RE teacher. She has taught in Glasgow and now lives in Leicester.

> I think the best way to live is to find true happiness. Not buy a new car or get drunk. You have got to find TRUE happiness from the inside of yourself because you will not find true happiness out of money, and even if you did, it will not last but true happiness will.
>
> *Michiko is a 12-year-old Buddhist girl*

Tibetan Buddhism

In this article, Robin Jackson examines some of the key teachings of his own school of Buddhism, relating them to some ways of presenting Buddhism in the classroom.

My religion

By way of establishing some context, I should point out that the tradition of Buddhism that I belong to is the Karma Kagyu school of Tibetan Buddhism, although my community, uniquely I think, has an equally strong connection with the Sakya school.

None of this may be of any interest to a non-specialist readership, but I think it is very important that I make clear that I cannot speak for, or hope to represent, other Buddhist traditions other than by expressing the fundamental teachings that all traditions share.

Tibetan Buddhism is essentially 'vajrayana' Buddhism. To understand where this fits into the 'Big Picture', I will explain how the Tibetans understand how the different 'vehicles' of Buddhism relate.

Tibetans understand Buddhism to be divided into two main categories:
- **Hinayana** or 'small vehicle';
- **Mahayana** or 'greater vehicle'.

Hinayana is supposed to represent the teachings given by the Buddha which have been preserved in the Tripitaka or Pali Canon. These include all the basic teachings about karma, samsara, the three marks of existence and the four noble truths, and so on.

The mahayana differs from the hinayana in two ways:
- understanding of reality;
- the ultimate goal.

Firstly, mahayana philosophy extends the hinayana understanding of anatta (meaning the 'non-self' of the individual), to mean that all phenomena lack inherent 'self nature'. This is the teaching called 'emptiness'.

Secondly, Tibetans see the goal of the hinayana schools as characterised (some might say unfairly) as striving for 'self-liberation', whilst the mahayana goal is to aspire to become like the Buddha himself by resolving to gain enlightenment for all beings. This resolution is called bodhicitta. One who takes this vow is called a bodhisattva (one who is destined for enlightenment).

The mahayana can also be divided into two:
- the ordinary mahayana;
- the extraordinary mahayana – the vajrayana – the 'diamond vehicle'.

The path of the ordinary mahayana accumulates the conditions for buddhahood through perfecting six virtues of generosity, moral discipline, patience, effort, meditation and wisdom itself.

The extraordinary mahayana or the vajrayana contains extremely skilful and powerful techniques through which one is able to achieve the aim of complete enlightenment for others far more swiftly than if one were to follow the six perfections of the ordinary mahayana. These teachings come from the scriptures called 'tantras' and hence it is sometimes referred to as 'tantric' Buddhism. The vajrayana is a further dimension of the mahayana and in no way contradicts it.

> Being determined to accomplish the supreme benefit for all sentient beings, who are more valuable than a wish-fulfilling gem, I will hold them very dear.
>
> *From the* Eight verses of mind training *by Geshe Langri Thangpa (1054–1123)*

> Just as the trunk of an ordinary tree, Lying in the sandalwood forests of the Himalayas, Absorbs the perfume of sandal from the moist leaves and branches, So you come to resemble whomever you follow.
>
> *Patrul Rinpoche (nineteenth century)*

The original inspiration of my Buddhist tradition – the significance of our history

The Tibetans' view of the foundation, development and expansion of Buddhism differs markedly from the Theravada. For example, we believe that the Buddha was already enlightened before he appeared in his historical form. We believe that the Mahayana sutras were not taught at a separate time to the Theravada sutras, but that the Buddha's teachings were perceived differently by different disciples in dependence upon their aptitude. Therefore the normal presentation of Buddhism as it is commonly set out in textbooks and other academic works is not accepted by many Tibetan scholars.

Historically, Buddhism came to Tibet in the seventh century CE. It was King Songsten Gampo who initiated the first wave of translations. The Tibetan script was based on the Sanskrit and the language itself was greatly influenced by Buddhist concepts. Hence it became perfectly suited to communicating subtle concepts with great accuracy.

Padmasambhava (known by Tibetans as Guru Rinpoche – the 'precious Guru') ensured the success of Buddhism. He was said to be the 'second Buddha', the tantric counterpart to Shakyamuni. It was Padmasambhava who 'tamed' the local deities and bound them to protect the dharma. Some people interpret this to mean that he was able to tame the local Bon priests who represented the original spiritual tradition in Tibet and were politically influential at the time.

By the time of the ninth century the monasteries were destroyed by the new king, Lang Dharma, and Buddhist monastic practice disappeared. Lay people still continued to practise, but over the years much of what was practised became perverted and Buddhism appeared to lose its 'purity'.

A second wave of transmission from India to Tibet started in the eleventh to fourteenth centuries CE, and this was a time of great spiritual zeal in Tibet. The founder of the Kagyu tradition was Marpa Lotsawa (1012–1097) who travelled to India to receive teachings from the Indian masters. He passed this on to his famous disciple the poet Milarepa (1040–1123) and he to his disciple Gampopa (1079–1173). Gampopa transmitted the teachings of Marpa to his disciple Dusum Khyenpa (1110–1193) who became the first Karmapa – the head of the Karma Kagyu School. From then on the Karmapa is said to have taken rebirth as the next Karmapa to continue his work. The present Karmapa is the seventeenth in this line.

I mention this detailed history to point out the paramount importance of history in our tradition. The teachings we receive are exactly the same teachings that Marpa received from his gurus in India, who had themselves received them from enlightened beings. The teachings gain their power and efficacy from the strength of the lineage. Each teaching bears its own lineage which is traced with great care from disciple to master back to the original source. Only one who has been authorised by his master to teach may pass the particular teaching on to his disciples.

Tibetans spend a long time studying the history and tradition of each teaching they study; before or after each teaching received, a lama will explain where he received the teaching from and where this teaching originated so that his disciples can be sure that it has an authentic lineage.

My lama uses the analogy of the leaf and the tree to help explain the importance of lineage: a leaf on its own is liable to be blown by the winds hither and thither as it is not rooted deeply. However the tree itself, because it is so firmly rooted, remains firm and strong. Likewise, teachings that originate in the minds of contemporaries are weak compared to the teachings that have been practised in an unbroken lineage for thousands of years.

In Vajrayana Buddhism the teacher or 'lama' plays an absolutely critical role, it is his or her instructions that guide the disciple to Buddhahood. But they are only effective

> Noble One
> you should think of
> yourself as someone
> who is sick,
> Of the dharma
> as the remedy,
> Of your teacher
> as a skilful doctor
> And of diligent
> practice as the way
> to recovery.
>
> The Sutra Arranged
> Like A Tree

> Not to examine the
> lama,
> Is like drinking
> poison,
> Not to examine the
> disciple,
> Is like leaping from
> a precipice.
>
> *Padmasambhava
> (eighth century)*

as long as the disciple has complete faith in them as embodying the enlightened state itself. This absolute confidence in the master must arise from a rigorous examination of the credentials of the master as well as of the student. As Patrul Rinpoche says, 'Since you place all your trust in your lama, to rely on a false spiritual friend without examining him properly is like approaching a venomous snake coiled beneath a tree thinking it is just the tree's cool shadow.'

Essentially a vajrayana master must be endowed with compassion and mindfulness, be free from pride, ignorance, spite or hatred. He or she must hold an unbroken lineage of vajrayana teachings and have achieved realisation of them. He or she must also be learned in the general teachings of all Buddhist traditions.

Throughout the ages 'gurus' have misused their position of power and so a rigorous approach to this most trusting of relationships is vital.

Tibetan Buddhism worldwide today

Tibetan Buddhism has been dealt a serious blow since the middle of the last century. Not only is its homeland flooded by the Chinese but corruption is spreading throughout the monasteries. It is actually quite a depressing state of affairs. Monks in Nepal can be seen cavorting with their female Western sponsors, pocketing large sums of money in return for some 'secret teachings'. However one blessing is that Tibetan Buddhism has been forced to travel. This means that the situation we find in the West is similar to the situation Tibet was in in the eleventh century. At that time Buddhism was being perverted as teachings were forgotten or misinterpreted. Buddhism in its homeland of India was slowly disappearing. Translators were sent from Tibet to receive the teachings in their purest form. In the West today there are many different groups who claim to be practising Buddhism, but have merely reinterpreted the teachings. Tibetans believe that the teachings should be adhered to without interpretation.

Tibetan Buddhism in the UK today

Obviously Buddhism is becoming a popular religion in the UK. This is partly due to the fact that people perceive Buddhism to be a more 'rational' religion since it is 'atheistic'. I think this appeals to a lot of people who are disillusioned with Christianity. This has led some people to say that Buddhism is not a religion. I think this is palpably untrue, as it fulfils all the characteristics of a religion that Ninian Smart sets out for example. Just belief in God does not a religion make. Tibetan Buddhism requires faith in deities, has pilgrimages, holy books, religious leaders, forms of ritual worship, ethical prescriptions, monastic communities, spiritual art forms and so on.

Tibetan Buddhism among the religions

Respect for others is the very backbone of our faith. This is the epitome of selflessness. Some people today fancy a 'pick and mix' religion. My lama refers to this as 'Jamie Oliver spirituality': a little bit of this and a little bit of that. None of my teachers have any respect for this. If you have a tradition you must follow it properly. Even within Buddhism itself there are strict guidelines about the path that you must follow. So 'new' ways of trying to combine Buddhism with forms of Hindu yoga or trying to fuse Buddhist philosophy with scientific inquiry are ineffective.

The Buddha is quoted as saying, 'I do not mind who they are as long as their words are endowed with wisdom'. There is beauty in every tradition that espouses loving kindness. The Dalai Lama has said that those who practise Christianity will be reborn in heaven, those who are Hindus will be reborn in whatever realm they pray for and Buddhists are striving for Nirvana.

> The dharma is nobody's property. It belongs to whoever is the most interested.
> *Patrul Rinpoche (nineteenth century)*

> If having found these freedoms, I do not practise what is good, Nothing could be more mistaken, Nothing could be more stupid!
> *Shantideva (eighth century)*

Human life: its value

Human life is regarded as 'precious' since it is the ground and foundation of enlightenment. It is rare and is unstable. It is only as a human that one can become enlightened since it is only as a human that one has the space to be able to observe, analyse and become aware of one's own mind. As a hell being, ghost or animal the suffering is too intense to consider liberation. As a god, life is too blissful to bother thinking about wanting to escape samsara.

For a life to be considered a precious human life, it must be endowed with the eight freedoms and ten endowments:

The eight freedoms – these constitute a birth free from the following negative situations:

- Birth in hell;
- Birth as a hungry ghost;
- Birth as an animal;
- Birth as a god;
- Birth as a human with defective senses (that stop them from hearing or understanding the dharma);
- Birth as a human at a time without the Buddha's teachings;
- Birth as a barbarian;
- Birth as a human possessing wrong views (for example, that there is no karma).

The ten endowments:

- To be born as a human;
- To possess undamaged senses;
- To live in a country in which dharma is practised;
- To have faith in the basic teachings of dharma (Karma, four truths, and so on);
- To have not committed the five heinous crimes (killing one's mother or father, killing the lama, and so on);
- A Buddha has appeared;
- He taught the dharma;
- The dharma still endures;
- There are other practitioners;
- There are others with compassion who support the practice of dharma.

Hence it is taught that a precious human life must have all these factors present. It is thus extremely rare. However it is also taught that whilst death is certain, its time is uncertain. Consequently the Buddhist is spurred into action by understanding the great potential they have as well as the fragility of it.

Two analogies for the value of human life

A blind turtle surfaces once every 100 years in an ocean the size of the Earth. The chance of that turtle putting its head through a hoop floating on the ocean, tossed by the wind is greater than that of achieving a precious human birth. Human birth and life are thus of immense rarity and value.

If a jewel trader should sail to an island that was covered with jewels, where the sand was gold dust and the rocks lapis lazuli, he would be incredibly stupid to leave the island with nothing. He should gather as much as he can before setting sail again.

Likewise, born as a human, one should use the opportunity to try to achieve liberation; to act otherwise would be incredibly stupid.

This helps a Buddhist really appreciate the present moment, since in the next moment they may have lost this opportunity.

> Now while there is freedom to act, I should always present a smiling face And cease to frown and look angry: I should be a friend and counsel to the world.
>
> *Shantideva (eighth century)*

> The Buddha has said that it is as hard to become a human, As for a turtle to put its head through the hole of a yoke, Tossed about on the waters of a great ocean.
>
> *Shantideva (eighth century)*

An inspiring leader today

Lama Jampa Thaye is one of very few Westerners to be authorised as a fully qualified lama. He is able to give Vajrayana empowerments. He is extremely careful to preserve the purity of dharma and is unwilling to make any compromises at all. The community which he organises is very traditional, whilst still fundamentally English. There is no liberalising of the teachings, it has not been westernised and yet he advises strongly against anyone trying to become Tibetan. The idea is that Tibetan Buddhism will eventually become English Buddhism, but only if great care is taken in the translation of texts and the maintenance of the strict vows and pledges a Vajrayana practitioner must keep.

Lama Jampa Thaye stresses the importance of maintaining a normal working life. It is difficult to maintain one's practice as well as work. Both take up so much time! They appear to be mutually exclusive, but the idea is that dharma should permeate every aspect of life. There is never a situation when one cannot practise patience or loving kindness!

Robin Jackson

Robin Jackson has been studying and practising Buddhism for ten years. He is head of Religious Education at Fallibroome High School and recently married his wife Helen. Combining the three is not as easy as it sounds!

How can we ensure that the Buddhism that is taught in schools is authentic?

In this contribution, Gary Beesley suggests principles for those who represent Buddhism in the classroom which both RE professionals and Buddhists might hold dear. He looks for teaching of Buddhism which eradicates what is not pure, which is willing to learn, which is well informed and which is inclusive.

Certain preliminaries utilised within the Tibetan Buddhist tradition in the development of proper meditative understanding might equally be utilised by individuals and authorities charged with ensuring authenticity in the teaching of Buddhism in schools. These preliminaries involve the eradication of impurities within the mind of the meditator, alongside the cultivation of certain qualities.

In educational circles, an arbitrary sub-division of the classification of 'impurities' to be eradicated could be 'intransigence' and 'misinformation'. These can be illustrated by example:

Intransigence

A scheme of work for teaching RE to 11–14s published by the government's English Qualifications and Curriculum Authority (QCA), in a unit on Buddhism, posed the question 'How helpful are the ten precepts for Buddhists when having to decide what to do?' The page features presently at the Standards Site, a seemingly well informed and authoritative resource endorsed by a government agency.

An eminent colleague wrote to a senior figure within the QCA explaining that the principal moral practice of all orthodox Buddhists, lay and ordained, was maintenance of not ten but five precepts or panchasila, and further, that the ten precepts were actually only practised by a comparative minority, in preparation for full ordination, or by lay people of particular traditions on certain festival days. Since the five precepts are practised almost universally amongst Buddhists, and since there is a

good deal of reference to them in existing educational literature, both my colleague and I felt that QCA had somewhat 'missed the mark' and therefore communicated with them, with the intention of rectifying an obvious mistake and in the hope of ensuring that teachers would be able to link the scheme of work to their available resources which refer, practically universally, to five precepts.

QCA's response was to state that, since *some* Buddhists practised observance of the ten precepts, they felt it unnecessary to act.

This unwillingness to act illustrates my first point, namely the intransigence of some who are, in a sense, 'subject guides'. The fact that the vast majority of Buddhists do not practise observance of the ten precepts, alongside the fact that nearly all references to a universally held code of moral conduct in the majority of available resources referred to the five precepts, was not enough to persuade those charged with ensuring authenticity to change. The resource remains online, and thus the misconception that a large proportion of Buddhists practise the ten precepts continues to be disseminated. Moreover, the confusion experienced by teachers of RE with other specialisms searching for resources to support the scheme of work remains.

My first point then is that, if they wish to present Buddhism to students as it exists within the Asian traditions, those in authority must be willing to rectify mistakes as and when they are informed of them, rather than assuming that status equals infallibility.

Misinformation

My second point relates, to a degree, to the first point. However, I have chosen to use a different example to illustrate its meaning.

Recently, while perusing a widely utilised examination awarding body's set of specimen GCSE papers and mark schemes, I came across the following definition of the Pali term 'bodhisattva' which has been variously translated elsewhere as 'enlightenment being', 'buddha-to-be' and 'one destined for enlightenment'. Bodhisattvas were here defined as 'beings who delay their own enlightenment to help others attain enlightenment'. Students who included this definition were actually awarded a higher-level mark than those who chose to define the term as 'a being who wants others to become enlightened'.

The principal problem with this higher-ranking definition is that it is wrong. A bodhisattva is actually someone who strives to achieve enlightenment in order to free others from suffering: such a motive drives the bodhisattva towards achieving his or her goal at the earliest opportunity, so as to alleviate the suffering of others as quickly as is possible; no bodhisattva would postpone their own enlightenment since it is from within that state that they can best benefit others.

The second problem with the definition is that it actually directly contradicts the true significance of the bodhisattva sentiment. It thus represents misinformation in one of its worst forms, wherein it is not simply incorrect but is the opposite truth of the matter.

It is to the credit of the examining board concerned that, when this issue was raised, they immediately agreed to take steps towards rectifying the mistake. However, the presence of the definition illustrates my second point, namely that, for whatever reasons, a number of inaccuracies have crept into educational resources over the years. The result is that incorrect information is being widely disseminated as fact. Similar mistakes appear throughout recently published resources in reference to Buddhist attitudes towards abortion and sexuality.

A simple remedy for this problem would be for those who guide the teaching of the subject to ensure that their sources and resources are reliable. While SACREs, examination boards, RE advisers and publishers may well have a number of differing priorities, it does not seem unreasonable to expect that authenticity should be one of them. Reliance upon expert advice and stringent checking of providers' histories, credentials and resources,

may seem somewhat draconian to some. The reality of the situation, however, is that if we wish to convey a clear and truthful picture of how genuine adherents actually practise, such measures are necessities. If we do not address this issue, then serious misconceptions concerning important aspects of Buddhist doctrine will become increasingly ingrained.

Inclusiveness

Referring back to our original model, as well as eradicating impurities, Buddhist practitioners striving for meditative perfection must also cultivate certain qualities. In educational circles, one important quality to be cultivated if we are to ensure the accurate teaching of Buddhism is that of inclusiveness.

Look at the contents page of any Buddhism textbook in schools and one is certain to find that the principal references relate to such topics as the three universal truths, the four noble truths, the noble eightfold path, the Theravada tipitaka, vipassana meditation, the monastic sangha and so forth. Similar formats appear in various examination board specifications.

The problem with taking the above concepts as the objects of focus when examining Buddhism and Buddhist practice is that they are actually only prominent within one of several of the orthodox Buddhist traditions. It would not be unusual for example, to find an experienced Tibetan Buddhist with a profound understanding of the deepest aspects of Buddhist philosophy who had never even heard of the three universal truths and the noble eightfold path.

Unfortunately, focusing solely on such topics as those outlined above creates the impression that this is what all Buddhists practise and believe. The upshot of this is that the richness and diversity of the Buddhist traditions is ignored, perpetrating a thoroughly partial view of what Buddhism actually is. Admittedly, one does find reference to other traditions, usually towards the back of the book. But these have the feel of having been added as an afterthought, as if the 'other' Asian Buddhist traditions are minority groups who practise a corrupt form of Buddhism. Nowadays, one is perhaps more likely to find reference to newly-arisen occidental Buddhist groups with no links to Asian traditions than one is to find reference to orthodox traditions with histories stretching back over hundreds of years, traditions that continue to be practised throughout the modern world by a significant number of individuals in the same way as they have been for centuries.

The fault is perpetuated at GCSE level where, on the one hand, it is claimed that candidates should be aware of 'the common ground that all Buddhists share' as well as 'the significant differences between them' while, on the other hand, when one examines syllabuses one finds that the technical language is Pali (the language of the Theravada) and the vast majority of the content relates to Theravadin doctrine and practice.

This is not an attempt to blacken the name of the noble Theravada, nor is it an attempt to apportion blame: the problem arises out of the limited research of our academic forefathers coupled with the assumption that their work represented a complete picture. Nevertheless, the situation has now changed; there is now available to us sufficient information concerning the diversity of the Buddhist traditions alongside accurate demographic knowledge for us to be able to reassess our teaching of the subject and the manner in which we portray the various traditions. Ignorance is no longer an excuse! If they are to accurately portray the multiplicity of the traditions in an inclusive and authentic manner, then those who produce resources, schemes of work and syllabuses must be encouraged not to look back at how the subject has been taught in the past, but around themselves, at the vast amount of accurate and fascinating information that is now available to them. In this way, we can ensure that the teaching of Buddhism in schools does justice both to learners and to the faith.

Gary Beesley

A lesson for 10-year-olds: Buddhism is a religion which encourages the enquirer to 'try it and see!'

The following extract is from Buddha's advice to the townspeople of Kalama who were confused by religious teachers who promoted their own doctrines and debunked those of others:

Come, Kalamas. Do not go by oral tradition, by lineage of teaching, by hearsay, by a collection of scriptures, by logical reasoning, by inferential reasoning, by reflection on reasons, by acceptance of a view after pondering it, by the seeming competence of a teacher, or because you think 'the ascetic is our teacher'. But when you know for yourselves, 'These things are wholesome, these things are blameless; these things are praised by the wise; these things if undertaken and practised, lead to welfare and happiness,' then you should engage in them.

The Kalamas Sutta (from the Anguttara Nikaya)

The concept of impermanence in Buddhism

Who am I? How am I different from a few years ago? What will I be like when I am older?

These questions belonging to everyone's 'personal search' are questions any adult might profit from asking themselves. They were posed to a large class of 10-year-olds at Worth Primary School in Poynton, a semi-rural village south of Manchester, as part of the work on Buddhism. The theme was the Buddhist concept of 'impermanence' which would then progress to learning about the four noble truths.

There were two sessions to introduce the concept: the first focused on 'change' and how the pupils had changed since babyhood and how they might like to change in the future; the second focused on introducing the Buddha as one who realised the impermanence of everything in the world. This was followed by creative work.

Aims and objectives

For pupils:

- to become aware of the world of change within which they live;
- to realise that it is possible to ask oneself questions about the past, present and future in one's life, and that one can influence the future for oneself and so enhance one's spiritual development;
- to appreciate that understanding impermanence is part of Buddhism;
- to enhance their own spirituality further by creating an art form showing 'impermanence'.

Teaching and learning: session 1

Pupils' answers to the questions in the title were used to write poetry which was displayed alongside objects they brought from home from their babyhood.

Teaching and learning: session 2

In discussion, the pupils were asked: What can you see around you that changes? Is there anything that doesn't change?

Initially, the pupils suggested that eyes, houses, personality were permanent but after discussion it was agreed that not even the sun was permanent. Padmasri, a member of The Western Buddhist Order from Clear Vision Trust, Manchester, introduced different Buddha rupas and the concept of impermanence. Various mudras or hand positions were considered and pupils suggested their own symbolic hand positions for friendship, determination and so on.

Body sculptures

In groups, pupils worked out body sculptures to show a shape or an object changing. They chose trees and plants growing, moving from childhood to old age and arguing and making friends. In spite of the large numbers, the pupils worked co-operatively and used the space between the desks effectively.

Art work

Pupils then represented the concept of 'impermanence' in art form. One boy used his technological skills to make an egg with a moving shell to reveal a chicken. Another made a clock with moving hands because he said, 'Time is impermanent'. One girl made a design of her name because she is called both Kate and Katie and she said her name is always changing. In clay, there were examples of cats and birds growing from babyhood to adulthood as well as a melting snowman.

The pupils were enthusiastic and involved. A measure of the success was when one pupil said to another, 'I don't want this afternoon to end.' Indeed it is the kind of phrase every teacher of RE hopes to hear at the end of any session.

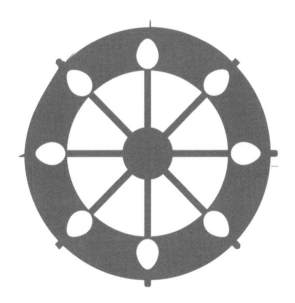

Helping teachers tackle my religion in the classroom:
Guidance from inside the Christian faith

> Jesus said, 'I am the true vine and my father is the gardener. I am the vine and you are the branches. If you remain in me you will bear much fruit.'
>
> *John's Gospel, chapter 15*

> Christianity is the 'world leader' in religious division. Catholic, Orthodox and Protestant divisions of the church are also sub-divided to an amazing degree – there are over 20,000 different Christian groups or denominations in the world.

Christianity – the vine and the branches

When you meet with a group of people from the same religion as yourself, you already know, just because you're all different people, that you won't explain or describe your faith in exactly the same way.

When four Christians sat down together to talk, we realised that it is not just our experiences and interpretations themselves which differ, but also the priorities which we assign to them. It was as if each of us was looking at our faith through a kaleidoscope, turning it gently to change the pattern a little and showing it to the next person.

Christianity is an 'organic' tradition – living and growing in the world today through the lives of those who embrace it, yet remaining rooted in its historical beginnings. Since the history itself is easily accessible from so many sources, we decided that the most useful thing for RE teachers would be to share something of the conversation that the four of us began to have together. In this way, we hope that RE teachers will grasp something of our belief that Christians are living branches attached to the vine which is Jesus (see John 15:1–17).

Who are we?

Andrew: I am a 22-year-old NQT teaching RS at The Bishop's Stortford High School, a large comprehensive for boys in Hertfordshire. The school and the Religious Studies Department both have a strong Christian ethos. I would place myself loosely within the Methodist tradition.

Sarah: I belong both to a Baptist church and to the inter-denominational West Midlands Anabaptist Study Group. I've taught RE for 12 years at Cockshut Hill – a mixed 11–18 comprehensive in Birmingham. With our mainly secular pupils we need to explore questions about religion in the world as a whole, and to offer opportunities for pupils' own spiritual reflection. Anti-racist education is an increasingly important part of our work.

Ann Marie: I have been RE Co-ordinator at St Thomas of Canterbury Blue Coat Church of England (Aided) Junior School for almost 8 years. Some of our children are from practising Christian families but the school primarily serves the local community. I was brought up as an Anglican and continue to attend the church where I was baptised and confirmed.

Paul: I have worked in mixed secondary Roman Catholic comprehensive schools since I started teaching 10 years ago. I have led RE departments of both subject specialists and non-specialists. I have responsibility for the school's moral and spiritual development, liturgical and acts of collective worship programme. I am also a Section 23 inspector for Westminster Diocese.

We felt it was important to share with each other at the outset what each of us considers to be the absolute core of our faith. So the first question we asked each other was:

What is at the spiritual heart of Christianity?

Andrew

For me, the reality that is central to the believer is belief in and experience of the Divine. This may be expressed as a systematic theological exposition or as a personal encounter. I will adopt the latter as all I can say of the Divine is that which I have encountered. I appreciate that this story differs from individual to individual, but this is my story.

To quote songwriter Eric Brazilian; 'What if God was one of us?' This is the question that for me reveals the spiritual heart of the Christian faith. Christian theology is essentially truth-seeking. As a Christian I am searching for God, attempting to discover what God may be like and then reacting to this discovery throughout my life. But this God is not some abstract unknowable mystery; God has become one of us. Jesus Christ is the revelation of what God is like.

Jesus told the parable of the 'pearl of great price' (Matthew 13:45–46), in which a man finds the perfect pearl, then goes and sells everything he has to buy it. Jesus is that 'pearl of great price'. He is the truth, the ultimate reality. God has become one of us. As a Christian I believe that I have had an encounter with this man Jesus Christ, it is a life-changing encounter that demands a response.

This response has been to embark upon a living relationship with God. In the words of Martin Smith, 'The wonder of it all, is that I am living just to fall more in love with you.' The relationship between God and his people is described in passionate terms in the love poetry found in Song of Songs 2:16: 'I am my beloved's and he is mine'. Christianity is never just a set of rules or moral teachings, and is not merely a set of beliefs and doctrines to accept. It is at its heart a relationship with a God who loves us, and (just like any lover) God wants us to love him in return. Revd Alfred Ackey (1887–1960) in his famous hymn describes this relationship:

'He lives, He lives, Christ Jesus lives today!
He walks with me and talks with me along life's narrow way.
He lives, He lives, salvation to impart!
You ask me how I know He lives?
He lives within my heart.'

Each individual will experience and respond to this in numerous different ways, but what unites many Christians is the experience of something worth living for, the pearl of great price. For me that response is to attempt to live a life that mirrors the life of Christ.

Paul

At the heart of the Christian faith is the offer of eternal life and salvation through Jesus Christ. Christians believe that Jesus is the 'incarnation', God who became a man, in order to restore the broken relationship, caused by sin, that existed between humans and God. The sacrifice of Jesus, his death and resurrection were necessary in order to reconcile us with God.

Sarah

Like Andrew, I cannot describe my faith without focusing on Jesus. The incarnation is like a jigsaw puzzle piece which lies right in the centre of the picture. So many other pieces fit onto it. Believing that Jesus understood totally what it was like to be human helps me to cope better with suffering, although I cannot fully understand it. It is as if the picture on the puzzle has worn off, yet we know the pieces must be right because they all fit together.

> **Christianity is Christ.**
> *GK Chesterton*

> **There is no Christianity without forgiveness.**
> *Robert Beckford*

> **'Christianity, if false, is of no importance. If true, it is of supreme importance. The one thing it cannot be is moderately important.**
> *CS Lewis*

> **We must not seek the child Jesus in the pretty figures of our Christmas cribs. We must seek him among the undernourished children who have gone to bed tonight without eating, among the poor newsboys who will sleep in the doorways.**
>
> *Archbishop Oscar Romero of El Salvador*

> **The church is like a bag of chips. Take it with a pinch of salt, but at its best it's brilliant.**
>
> *Anon*

Christianity is built upon a series of paradoxes. The mystery of a transcendent creator God whose ways are too difficult for us to understand is balanced by a love relationship with Jesus who taught us to call God 'Abba' (meaning Daddy). And those aspects of God which are mysterious to us become more understandable through the mediation of the Holy Spirit. That is why I think 'trinity' has to be another central piece of this theological jigsaw.

Christians don't all arrive at the same formula for expressing how they came to understand their faith. We may come to the 'fine pearl' after a long time of searching, or just 'happen upon' the treasure (Matthew 13:44). When the early church met in councils to sort out the fundamentals of the faith, there were many struggles as to how to express these paradoxes. This side of heaven I guess I have only a glimpse of the whole picture, and I may not be able to describe it very well, but I do know that it is a very great treasure indeed.

Ann Marie

Like Sarah says, we don't all express our faith in a neat formula. For me the heart of Christianity is linked with a feeling of 'belonging' in a church. As a child I was brought up within the Anglican faith but I also used to visit the local Roman Catholic church with my dad. There is a great deal of diversity amongst the churches in Britain today, and it is important that as an individual, a Christian is able to find a church where they feel they are able to express their beliefs with like-minded people. As an Anglican I enjoy the ritual of the services, the 'family' that I have grown up with, and the sense of peace I feel when entering the church. In my days as a student I encountered many other churches and worship groups but this is the place I feel most comfortable with and 'at home.'

We agreed that our experiences of our own denominations have been highly significant in the different ways we express the heart of our faith, and in our preferred styles of worship. Nonetheless, it is the sense of being rooted in the same tradition despite denominational differences that we would want to convey to those learning about Christianity in the RE context. This applies particularly when we seek to look outwards into the world as a whole and to embrace Christian values in our daily lives. So the next big question for discussion was:

What are the values and virtues that being a Christian inspires?

Sarah

What a huge question! I'd begin with the word 'inspires'. We read about God breathing life into humankind at the creation. I'm not a literalist in these matters, but I do believe in the truth of the idea that God created life for living! Jesus said that he had come so that we might have 'life in all its fullness' (John 10:10). Essentially, then, I think the values and virtues prized by Christianity must spring from the life of Jesus itself. And furthermore, they can never be a set of rules which become 'the death of us'.

For me, it's about discovering what Jesus is teaching me in all the different situations and relationships of life. There are some big principles that I can hold on to. These can also be found in the Old Testament prophets such as Amos and Hosea – principles such as 'loving kindness or mercy' (expressed in Hebrew as hesed) and 'peace or wholeness' (shalom). In the gospels I can see these ideals at work in the relationships Jesus had with all people. He also had compassion and patience. And of course, the message of the cross is one of forgiveness. So there are plenty of virtues and values there for me to embrace in seeking to live as a Christian. Like many Christians, when trying to work out how to act in different situations I ask myself, 'What Would Jesus Do?'

It's not always easy being a Christian! The values I've described are what I would call 'kingdom values'. They are what is important in God's realm. Living in the twenty-first century, in a wealthy country, I think it's easy to lose sight of kingdom values. The values of consumerism, exploitation, individualism to name but a few, push out compassion and so many others. For me, the call to live as a Christian is one which often involves swimming against the tide. Jesus turned the world upside down. There are countless places in the gospels where we see this (for example, Matthew 5–7, Mark 7:1–23, Luke 1:46–55, John 13:1–17). And what's more, I believe that Jesus came for all people, so justice, peace and mercy are things I must want actively for all people, whether they share my faith or not.

To sum it up, a quotation from one of my favourite Bible passages:

'Don't do anything from selfish ambition or from a cheap desire to boast, but be humble towards one another, always considering others better than yourselves. And look out for one another's interests, not just for your own. The attitude you should have is the one that Christ Jesus had.'

Philippians 2:3–5

Andrew

As Sarah has already suggested, the values and virtues of Christian living must spring from the life of Christ. The central virtue is one of unconditional love. Jesus demanded perfect standards but loved people no matter how sinful they appeared to be. The only things he had no time for were self-righteousness and hypocrisy. He declared the most important commandments to be 'love the Lord your God ... and love your neighbour as yourself' (Mark 12:30–31). In the parable of the sheep and the goats (Matthew 25:31–46), Jesus clearly states that those who follow him are those who selflessly give of themselves to help those rejected by society. We know what it means to love, but we so often attach conditions to it. Christ challenges us to give all with no thought of reward or gain, for the good of those who are in need (regardless of our own judgement as to whether they deserve our help or not).

Paul

The Christian faith presents a very real challenge in today's society. Christians are called through different ministries and vocations, whether they form part of the clergy, religious orders, communities or the laity to meet the challenges presented by contemporary secular society. Christians should approach these challenges in both prayerful and practical ways. Christians are urged to challenge injustice in today's world, wherever and in whatever form it may exist. Christians must accept the challenges that prejudice, discrimination, the denial of human rights, crime, violence and addiction offer and through their understanding and application of the gospel values should attempt reconciliation in society wherever possible.

Ann Marie

Indeed Jesus is at the centre of any Christian's life, and a virtue of this is that Jesus provides us with a role model of how we can live our lives as Christians. A value of this is that Jesus guides his followers and helps them throughout their daily life. Jesus is a friend who is always there to listen to you. He is someone I talk to each day and when I look back on past experiences, I can see how Jesus has guided me and helped me in my life.

We began to talk about our experiences of Christianity as children and young people. It was clear that none of us felt or wanted to perpetuate the idea that Christianity is all about people and events that happened 'long ago and far away'.

> From the cowardice that dare not face new truth,
> From the laziness that is contented with half truth,
> From the arrogance that thinks it knows all truth,
> Good Lord, deliver us.
>
> *Kenyan prayer quoted by Archbishop Desmond Tutu*

> People are often unreasonable, illogical and self-centred.
> Love them anyway.
> The good you do today, people will often forget tomorrow.
> Do good anyway.
> Give the world the best you have, and it will never be enough. Give the world the best you've got anyway.'
>
> *Based on Kent Keith's 'Paradoxical Commandments'*

How can we present Christianity as a living faith?

Ann Marie

Christianity is a religion of today and for the future. It is the inspiration for millions of people all over the world that helps them define how they live their lives, the decisions they make, and what they want from life. Therefore, it is important that Christianity is seen as a faith that is alive today and for teachers to identify living religious leaders, personalities and individuals. This may be famous people such as Mother Teresa of Calcutta, Jonathan Edwards or Kriss Akabussi, or it could be examples of individuals from a local community whose faith is a guiding force in their lives.

Pupils may encounter the Christian faith in many different ways:

- **In the home.** The values that are taught to children, the examples of role-models within the family or from friends.
- **Sunday School.** As an introduction to church, developing an understanding of Christian values, engaging with the stories, exploring their special relationship with Jesus.
- **Christian youth clubs**.
- **Denominational rites of passage**. Communion classes within the Anglican church where individuals meet to think through the commitment of confirmation and becoming an adult member of the Christian church.
- **Christian celebrations.** Celebrating key events in the calendar of the church such as Lent, Easter, Christmas and Epiphany.
- **Christian schools.** Schools that were founded by churches, which may still be partly funded by the church. Often such a school will have a strong relationship with its church, the teachers may be required to be practising Christians and the RE and acts of collective worship may be taught in relation to the Trust Deed.

I hope that Christian children in the future are able to feel positive about their personal identity and are able to express their beliefs confidently. I hope that they can respect and be sensitive to individuals from other faiths or those that have no faith.

Andrew

Christianity is, as Ann Marie has stated, a living vibrant faith. This is how it needs to be presented. However, I often find that the Christianity that I see presented and represented in society is far removed from the faith I experience. I constantly need to be reminded that the faith Jesus preached was a radical, controversial and unacceptable message that led to his crucifixion and the persecution of those who also lived out his message. This has now become the acceptable, comfortable, safe message of our nominally Christian society.

The message of Jesus is not simply a message to be believed, rather it is a message that firstly changes the individual and then causes them to work to change the world around them. It is lifestyle, it is to be lived 24/7. Jesus stated simply that 'Not everyone who calls me "Lord, Lord" will enter the Kingdom of heaven, but only those who do what my Father in heaven wants them to do' (Matthew 7:21).

For me the purpose of my faith is to live out what I pray in the Lord's Prayer. 'Our Father in heaven, hallowed be your name. **Your Kingdom come *on earth* as it is in heaven**.' My faith is a living one because it is about me attempting to help bring about the will of God on earth, here and now. In Matthew 25:45 the will of God is laid out as 'whenever you refused to help one of these least important ones, you refused to help me.'

> The second I met Mother Teresa, she struck me as being the living embodiment of moral good. Every moment her aim seemed to be 'how can I use this or that situation to help others?' She held my hand and said to me: 'I can do something you can't do, and you can do something I can't do. But we both have to do it.'
>
> *Bob Geldof*

> There are two poles in teaching Christianity: you can present it as about 4 decades of British decline, typified by empty grey old buildings, or as the biggest religion in the world: more people became Christian in the 1990s than in any decade ever. Good RE does both, and asks: why is it like this?

The last few years or so have seen the growth of youth movements which have increasingly aimed to do just this. The work of groups such as Soul Survivor, The Message, The Eden Project, The Tribe as well as organisations such as Greenbelt, Christian Aid, The Oasis Trust, are worth investigating as examples of how the Christian faith is being expressed as a living, life-changing faith.

Sarah

Like Andrew, I want pupils to be challenged by the radicalism of Jesus' life and teaching. Where there is a form of Christian nurture from the home or church, then pupils may, as Ann Marie herself did, feel comfortable and 'at home' in a particular denominational expression of Christianity. My pupils have not necessarily encountered Christianity in the ways that Ann Marie has suggested, but even if they have, the teenage years are often a time when people want to leave behind some of those aspects of belief and behaviour which they see as outdated or irrelevant. In the case of my own school, where specific Christian nurture is not appropriate, I want to be able to challenge pupils from Christian families to look again at the claims and demands of Christianity with a view towards making it their own living faith rather than merely an inherited one. I suppose this is analogous to pruning away at the branches in order to ensure continued growth. In relation to secular pupils and those of other faiths it can never be appropriate for RE teachers to have an evangelistic role, but, as a believer, I do want pupils to grasp something of what my faith means for my life. In my case it is more about trying to communicate something of the values and virtues I spoke about earlier rather than to teach about the phenomenology of the Christian religion.

Given the statutory provision that RE Agreed Syllabuses must include Christianity, we wanted to talk about some of the reasons why we feel it to be important. Using a framework with which RE teachers will be familiar, our discussion examined the following two questions:

What might pupils learn *about* Christianity, and what might pupils learn *from* Christianity?

Paul

I spoke earlier about the 'offer' which lies at the heart of the Christian faith. With this particular 'offer' in mind, a distinctively Christian religious education (in contrast to catechesis or evangelisation) suggests aims that are simple and yet profound. The offer is open to pupils of all faiths or none and is based on the following:

* A knowledge and understanding of the Christian faith and life;
* A knowledge and understanding about the response of Christian believers to the question of God and relationships to human life;
* The necessary skills appropriate to the pupils' age and capability to engage in critical examination and reflection on religious belief and practice.

A study of Christianity allows pupils the opportunity to develop a knowledge and understanding of God, Jesus Christ, the Bible, the church and the Christian way of life.

Studying Christianity should encourage pupils to develop appropriate skills; for example, ability to listen, think critically, spiritually, ethically and theologically. Studying Christianity should foster appropriate attitudes; for example, respect for truth, respect for the views of others, awareness of the spiritual, of moral responsibility, and of religious commitment in everyday life. These skills and attitudes have their place and provide the academic context of Christianity as a subject with school credibility. Alongside this is the responsibility to develop the spiritual dimension. It

> Children in the church are sometimes treated as if their only usefulness will be to keep things going in 30 years' time. But in the Bible, God often uses the young to chuck out all the rubbish that traps the current generation.

> Anyone can learn from Jesus, not just the Christians:
> Jesus was like some terrible moral huntsman, digging mankind out of the snug burrows in which they had lived hitherto. In the white blaze of this kingdom of his there was to be no property, no privilege, no pride, nor precedence; no motive indeed and no reward but love. Is it any wonder that men were dazzled and blinded and cried out against him?
> *HG Wells, science fiction writer and atheist*

would be meaningless for pupils to gain academic excellence through a study of Christianity if they remained spiritually void.

In the case of Christian pupils themselves, and in a Christian school, a study of Christianity should develop pupils' sense of moral responsibility, give them the ability to distinguish between right and wrong, between good and evil and give them the confidence if necessary to stand up and be counted! A study of Christianity should enrich the pupils' faith, inform them of their faith and enable them to put it into practice. With this in mind, learning from Christianity should transcend the classroom and permeate throughout the life of the whole school.

Is the study of Christianity only accessible to Christian students? In order to assess what the value of studying Christianity might be, a key question for teachers to ask is 'How has studying Christianity changed anything about my pupils?' I am not suggesting that pupils who have studied Christianity in school will be any better than those who have not (in either the academic or behavioural context), nor am I suggesting that teachers need to enter into the debate about whether morality is dependent on religion. I do think teachers should be regularly engaged in monitoring pupils' academic needs alongside their spiritual development when assessing what exactly can be learned from studying Christianity.

Andrew

There are three themes from what Paul has said that sum up for me what can be learned from Christianity. The first is that the study of Christianity (as with any religion) must transcend the classroom. This is essential because Christian theology is an attempt to identify what is true, and then in the light of this answer the question 'therefore on what principles should I live every day of my life?' It is not merely an academic discipline, but a matter of life, meaning and direction.

The second is the ability to consider matters of eternal significance. As Paul says above, 'At the heart of the Christian faith is the offer of eternal life and salvation through Jesus Christ.' This, if true, has massive and possibly shattering implications for each and every individual who hears this statement. This leads to reflection on the nature of truth, eternal salvation and then the appropriation of that truth for oneself. It is this that Christianity revolves around.

Thirdly, the challenge from Christian ethics is simply: what does it mean to actually live out our beliefs? At this point spirituality becomes intensely practical in nature. This leads to a holistic approach to faith, truth, identity and action. Thus what can be learned from Christianity is what it means to attempt to live as a complete person in what can be a fragmented world.

This has been an interesting project! The four of us found it challenging to express our ideas knowing that we could each only truly represent our own positions, both theologically and educationally, yet knowing that readers might regard us as representative of our denominations. In one sense, these 'branches' of the Christian church are highly significant, and the historical forces which shaped them are fascinating in themselves. Yet as a group of Christians we would each want to lay more emphasis on what unites us, on what we share, than on any differences between us. Above all, the image of each individual Christian as a part of the living vine, which is Jesus, is the one which we hold most dear.

The final word from us comes from Paul:

Pupils, aware of the historical context of Christianity and its development both locally and globally, must appreciate that Christianity is a living religion and is alive and well in the twenty-first century.

> Fellowship is heaven, and lack of fellowship is hell.
> *William Morris*

Helping teachers tackle my religion in the classroom
Guidance from inside the Hindu faith

In this article, the work of four teachers who come from different starting points within Hindu traditions or Sanatan Dharma – Jay Lakhani, Carol Tibbs, Naina Parmar and Neera Vyas – is woven together. Authentic voices do not all say exactly the same things, but teachers of RE will find value in the diversity of the voices blended here.

Authentic Hindu voices

Carol: I was attracted to Hinduism over 20 years ago, initially through meditation, chanting and hatha yoga, and became more involved with it after meeting my Guru. I spent several years in India, and have an MA in Hindu Studies from the School of Oriental and African Studies (SOAS) in London. I have just retired as head of Religious Studies in a comprehensive school in London, and plan to spend some more time in India! I have also been involved with teacher training and professional development, specifically focusing on Hinduism.

Naina: I was born in East Africa and grew up in Birmingham. I now live in London. I am a Farmington Fellow and currently work as a teacher supporting ethnic minority achievement, as well as co-ordinating RE and History in my primary school. I am involved with teachers' professional development training to improve RE and the teaching of Hinduism.

Neera: I was born in Kenya; grew up in Coventry; studied philosophy and theology at Heythrop College, London. I have taught RE for 10 years and feel Wales is my spiritual home, where I now teach part-time so that I can enjoy the glorious countryside, write and develop skills in complementary therapies. I have been head of RE in schools in Wrexham and Birmingham, am a member of the PCfRE national Executive and examiner for Welsh Joint Education Committee.

Jay: I have a Masters degree in theoretical physics from Imperial and Kings Colleges, London. I help run the Vivekananda Centre in London. We currently have fourteen classes teaching Hinduism at all levels in the UK. We are the largest body involved in Hindu education in the country.

The diversity of Hinduism as a strength

One of the problems that teachers have with Hinduism is its diversity. This can make it difficult to teach. We felt, however, that this diversity was a strength which allows great freedom of expression of spirituality. Diverse ideas can exist side by side, be respected and still be acceptable within the 'Hindu' framework. This is extended also to other religions, which are accepted as valid religious paths. For most Hindus, it is not so important which path you follow to develop spiritually, but that you do follow a path. Therefore there is a natural appreciation of most varieties of religious expression. This does not make it woolly but because it has developed over thousands of years it has absorbed many different ideas and expressions. There is, nevertheless, a unity that holds them all together. It is like a vast spectrum of ideas, beliefs and practices, and what a person does and believes depends on where they plug into this spectrum. Julius Lipner's image of the polycentric banyan tree is helpful in this respect also. Often apparent differences are simply different emphases. There may be ideas which appear diametrically opposed (and paradox is, in any event, something which does occur in religion) but there will still be common ground. There is no problem in these existing side by side. The teacher of RE needs to be aware that this will be reflected in a diversity of views in the classroom. So: no need to panic – try to be inclusive.

> What we call 'Hinduism' is not a unified and single entity, but the sum total of the traditional religious beliefs and practices of the Indian people, a colourful, diverse and complex set of traditions, inherited from a long history and sometimes only loosely related to one another.
>
> *T Patrick Burke*

> The difficulty of speaking of the divine:
> **He is the unseen see-er,
> the unheard hearer,
> the unthought thinker, the un-understood understander...
> He is the self within you,
> the inner controller,
> the immortal...**
>
> *Brihadaranyaka 3.7.23*

Concepts of God and ultimate reality in Hinduism

God with form

Hindus believe that one can think of God as a person (with shape) or one can think of him not as a person (without shape). It is like the example of ice and water. Ice takes on a shape but water does not seem to have any shape and yet they are both really the same thing. There is only one God but Hindus like to think of him or her in the form of their liking.

God as a person

It is easier to build a relationship with God if one thinks of the divine as a person. Some Hindus like to think of God as their real father in heaven. But why only as a father? Many Hindus like to think of God as their real 'mummy' in heaven. Hindus can choose the way they wish to think of God. The important thing is to love God. It makes no difference how one wishes to see him. One is allowed to pick and choose the way one thinks of God. Some like to think of him as Krishna. Some like to think of God as the Mother Goddess Durga – with many arms – holding many divine weapons. Some Hindus like to think of God as a little child. All these different ways to approach God are acceptable in Hinduism. There is only one God in Hinduism but one can choose the form.

God without form (but with qualities)

Some Hindus do not like to think of God having the shape of a man or woman. How can God be without any shape? We all believe in truth, love, power and such. None of these have any shape and yet we all believe in them. Hindus say that this is how one can think of God without shape. Some Hindus use fire as a symbol to think of God without any shape.

God beyond form and formless (Brahman)

These are not the only ways we can think of God. Hindus say that there are many more ways one can think of God.

If we concentrate and find out who we truly are, we find that 'we are really God'. This is very difficult to believe, but Hindus say that the 'real you' is called 'Atman' – God as your true self. That is why the greeting used by Hindus is: 'Namaste' – 'I bow down to God as you'. The highest worship of God is then thought to be 'service to mankind'. Hurting any living thing is considered wrong because it is the same as hurting ourselves.
Jay

> **Thou art the imperishable, the supreme object of knowledge;
> Thou art the ultimate resting place of this universe;
> Thou art the immortal guardian of the eternal law;
> Thou art the everlasting spirit.**
>
> *Bhagavad Gita, 11,18*

When we work in multi-faith classrooms, we feel we would have reservations about expressing this idea of 'God beyond form' in terms of 'you are God'. We prefer to refer to the 'oneness' of Atman and Brahman.
Carol and Naina

Worship

Worship is a popular topic in all key stages of Religious Education. The particular and unique contribution of Hinduism to any discussion on worship is the importance of the visual. That is not to say that this is always important to all Hindus, but it is certainly prevalent and prone to a great deal of misunderstanding. By trying to 'unpack' what is going on I have found a more sympathetic response from non-

Hindus. Even though the practices will never be acceptable to certain other religions, at least an understanding of the complexity underlying them fosters a respect and interest which might not otherwise be there. It is very hard to find the adequate words to convey what is happening because Hindu worship is very subtle. Here are some key points:

- Hindus do not worship idols. They worship God. Because of the connotations of the word 'idols' in other faiths the use of the word 'idols' should be avoided. The Oxford Dictionary defines the word 'idol' in two ways: 'false god' or 'image of deity used as object of worship'. Neither of these is a correct understanding of what happens in Hindu worship.

- There are many different aspects to a Hindu understanding of God (see previous section). I personally find that the image of white light refracted through a prism so that many different colours are visible is a good way to explain the relationship between the Absolute (Brahman) and the many different forms of God, usually spoken about as different gods and goddesses. It is said that God reveals him- or herself in different forms for the benefit of devotees. Everyone can, as Jay said, find the form that suits them. That form will determine where the devotee fits into the spectrum referred to in the introduction.

- Visual images assist worship in several ways:
  - They act as a focus in the same way as a photograph of an old friend might – prompting memories of character, events or stories, and feelings.
  - There are accepted scriptural guidelines as to the way each deity is represented. They must be recognisable. Each image includes symbols which say something about that particular aspect of God.
  - There is more than simply this – whether statues or pictures, because of the awareness that their content is sacred.
  - A worshipper might not necessarily be readily able to explain everything that is brought to mind by a particular image. They will have grown up with the stories and the symbols and these are so deeply ingrained in the subconscious that the effect and impact of the image or murti is instantaneous.
  - Before a statue is acceptable as a focus of worship in a mandir, it must go through a detailed process. It is usually (but not always) made by skilled craftsmen who have learned their trade through their families, going back hundreds of generations and following scriptural guidelines. Rituals and prayer form a regular part of this process. Finally, it must go through a special ritual of installation in the mandir, culminating in God's presence being invited into it. This is an extremely sacred moment and is often referred to as 'enlivening' or 'establishing the sacred breath'. I have personally witnessed this and I have no doubt that there is a marked change. Only then is it considered to be an acceptable focus for worship. Does this sound like an 'idol'? Maybe, but what is it that is being worshipped? It is still not the stone or brass (although some traditions may say that the stone or brass is itself transformed). What is alive is God's presence especially strongly in the form or 'murti'.

Regular prescribed worship must then be maintained. The murti will be anointed with special pure substances; dressed in beautiful clothes made or donated by worshippers as a means of showing their devotion; food should always be offered to God in thanks before eating. This is done by placing a sample in front of the murti while prayers are said. This is not 'feeding' the murti. The food is then considered to have been blessed and can be shared among devotees as prasad. In addition, arati (an act of worship involving the waving of lights) will be carried out at regular times. Those Hindus who have murtis installed in their homes may carry out a similar activity. In many ways it is like looking after a child, a practice to which most people can relate. It allows a devotee to express their love for God in

> Hindus believe that there is one God, one supreme being called Brahman. Hindus also believe that Brahman can be pictured and thought about in many different forms. This shows the power and presence of God, who is believed to be everywhere. This is why Hindus worship Brahman through many gods and goddesses.
>
> *Dilip Kadodwala*

> From the unreal,
> lead me to
> the real.
> From darkness,
> lead me to light.
> From death lead
> me to immortality.
>
> *A key Hindu prayer from the Upanishads*

a very intimate way. Nevertheless it is still not the stone or brass that is worshipped but God.

- Darshan. This literally means the reciprocal idea of seeing and being seen, in the sense that we might use the expression 'I see' meaning 'I understand'. It also has the meaning of 'being in the presence of divinity'. There is an interactivity between worshipper and God. The murti is observed closely, every aspect of it being appreciated, which directs all the senses into worship and away from the mundane (as does arati). When the shrine curtains are drawn back to reveal a murti, it is a very dramatic moment, which can cause devotees to gasp and drop to the floor, bowing in awe at being in the presence of God. At the same time, they feel their own presence and devotion acknowledged. Intense expression of humility and love might not be so easy without a form on which to focus.

- Arati. It is important to show how the items used in this form of worship function by disengaging all the senses from mundane stimuli and turning them towards God. The senses of touch, smell, sight, hearing and taste are not negated but transformed. This is a common idea in Hinduism.

I wouldn't expect teachers to cover anything like this amount of detail in the classroom with younger children, but I do feel that to have this background would inform and facilitate more confidence in dealing with the topic. There are, of course, many more points which could be made about worship, but I think this is the main one which is open to misinterpretation.

Carol writes:

This classroom activity for primary or secondary RE works well, and represents the Hindu traditions in an interesting way. It is worth integrating the 'design and make' aspect of the project with Design Technology lessons.

Make pujas (shrines) – individually or in groups – making it clear that this is an educational exercise. I have done this with secondary pupils in groups and it has worked so well that those in the previous year who didn't do it were very resentful!

Use a video or poster or set up a prototype arati tray using artefacts so that a list of all the items required can be made.

Materials

Some reasonably-sized boxes, coloured tissue paper, tinsel, cardboard and so on to decorate the box, and make flowers, decorations and the requisite items. In my experience pupils have better ideas about this than teachers and utilise all their CDT skills! They can label the items and explain their purpose.

This covers AT1 and AT2. The concentration, care and energy the pupils expend patiently putting the thing together, and the great sense of satisfaction at the end, allows the teacher to draw an analogy with the feelings Hindus might have caring for their pujas every day. The pupils learn a great deal about Hindu worship, and can better appreciate why this form of worship means so much to a Hindu.

As an alternative, pupils could make individual 'shrines' for something that is 'special' to them. This can lead to an exploration of the language of worship, sacredness and the 'special' and a thoughtful comparison of the lives of Hindus and the lives of other children in a class.

> We have a shrine
> at home to Ambaji,
> and my mum
> prays and makes
> offerings for us
> first thing every
> morning. We light
> the candles and
> sing together, and
> we remember that
> we are protected
> and loved. Life
> seems right with
> worship, and wrong
> without it.
>
> *Smita, aged 11*

Morality in the Sanatan Dharma: values and virtues in Hindu communities

Naina writes:

My personal experience of RE on Hinduism at school was largely embedded in historical attitudes and beliefs that Hinduism was idolatrous, barbaric and highly confusing, the complete opposite of what I experienced and identified with at home. I grew up feeling quite embarrassed to even identify myself with my faith and the general stereotypes associated with it. I later realised that Hindu teachings were more implicit than explicit. Hence the gap between school RE and what I was taught at home. RE teachers have often told me that it is one of the most difficult faiths to teach. Many are dissatisfied with current resources and reluctant to cause offence. It is often the safer options that emerge, such as focusing only on festivals, celebrations and rituals. Very little philosophising takes place.

In RE, as a teacher who is also a Hindu, I aim to share my own tradition; a treasure I have discovered that I hope will help fellow teachers in their delivery of the subject. Some of the points may be part of the common core of the religion, whilst some may be specific to my own tradition.

I have been drawn to the Bhakti Yoga tradition within Vaishnavism (the worship of Vishnu). This is one of the four main schools of thought and relates closely to my childhood experiences. I am very much inspired by the teachings of the Bhagavad Gita (translated by AC Bhaktivedanta Swami, 1983), which has helped me to appreciate that humans have the potential to realise their spiritual connection with God in their own way through the paths they follow. This releases me from criticism and judgement of other people's preferred life stances. As a teacher, I constantly strive to aim to provide an inclusive curriculum valuing pupils' varying and preferred learning styles so why can't the same be true with spiritual paths? For example, although I follow monotheism, the belief in one supreme God, I do not believe it is morally justified to say my path is superior and anything else is inferior. Ethically this attitude is not only narrow, but also judgemental. I often use the analogy with pupils that all around the world people have many names for the sun: sol, surya and soon, yet in actuality none can claim ultimate ownership, suggesting their sun is the best as there is only one sun. The way we see, experience and name the sun may vary, yet it still remains the same sun. Sanatan Dharma similarly views other faith paths in this way.

Bhakti (devotional) yoga promotes the idea that your faith and how you connect and serve God is not separate from your daily practice in life. This is known as dharma or one's duty. My duties vary according to which role I serve in. As humans we serve our families, our work, our friends through various reciprocal relationships, for example, in my case, whether I am a wife, a mother, friend, teacher, colleague or an employee, it is the way I behave (the values and virtues I imbibe) in these roles, which indicate my real spiritual integrity. I cannot claim to seek spiritual realisation or possess values and virtues if my work is shoddy or I do not behave with professional integrity. My spiritual advancement is directly affected by the way I live my daily life and the way I think, speak and treat people. In honesty, I aspire to do my duty well though I know I have a long way to go.

In terms of emotional intelligence, emotional literacy and self-awareness the Gita analyses three levels of varying consciousness or mental states in all of us called 'gunas'. These are light, fire and darkness. Each word symbolises our emotions and how we may feel and behave – happy, generous, angry, lazy and so on. These emotions are triggered by our own feelings and the environment or dealings around us. The Gita suggests and gives practical guidance on how to steady our consciousness to overcome excessive emotional states.

As a child, I was surrounded by people who could chant in the purest Sanskrit and explain the meaning in the simplest form. It was usual for me to wake up to my mother singing traditional hymns as she went about her morning chores. There was a smell of incense in the house, the atmosphere was pure and energising. My mother undertook the daily worship in the house but everyone, from my 70-year-old grandfather to the servant who came in to help with the household chores, went to the room that housed our small mandir and asked for God's blessings before doing anything.

Smruti, Hindu primary school teacher

> **Lord Krishna speaks:**
> **I deem most disciplined men of enduring discipline who worship me with a true faith entrusting their minds to me.**
> *Bhagavad Gita*

As a teacher, knowing this has helped me to become more aware of my mental state and that of others. I have found this helpful for my own self-awareness and of those around me. It helps me to recognise and become aware of stereotyping or labelling a child; distinguishing the difference between the trigger and the child. The Bhagavad Gita guides me to deliver my job, to be a teacher who aims to be inclusive, use positive reinforcement, avoid becoming too judgemental and possibly manage behavioural issues better.

The most commonly held and widely known Hindu concepts – karma, reincarnation and ahimsa (nonviolence) – are underpinned by deeper philosophical understanding which promotes greater self-awareness. It is a way of life; values and virtues are easier to imbibe when one realises one takes birth over and over again, and how to avoid it. We have the challenge of free will and we decide our destiny by the way we behave, speak and act. Karma, in short, suggests that every action, good or bad, has implications. I feel empowered that I alone take responsibility for my own destiny.

This can be broken down further into four stages. The analogy of planting and growing a seed demonstrates the meaning of karma clearly:

1 The seed (the desire).

2 The bud (the mind coming to a decision).

3 The fruit (performing the activity).

4 The harvest (the reaction: happiness or distress).

To some extent, everything depends on desire, the choices we make. Hindus believe pious activities lead one to become a better person. Here are some statements of truths and their application, related to Hindu philosophy, that I have found helpful in providing excellent opportunities for promoting discussions and debates in the classroom. It is an awareness of these that promotes morality, values and virtues in a practical way.

Statement A

There are three types of distress or suffering all humans experience until they attain liberation: freedom from the cycle of birth, death, old age and disease (samsara).

> Suffering or disturbances from our own mind and body;

> Suffering or disturbances from other living entities (humans, insects, animals);

> Suffering and disturbances caused by nature (floods, hurricanes, rain, snow, earthquakes and the like).

Statement B

All living beings have the tendency to possess four defects to some degree:

> To make mistakes: 'to err is human';

> To cheat: to propagate falsehood including even the odd white lie;

> Illusion: accepting as real something that is not;

> Imperfect senses: our senses are limited and can easily be misled.

Statement C

Knowing all beings have these defects, the four pillars of religion help to overcome them:

> **Truthfulness**: One should not distort the truth for some personal interest. Pursue an honest livelihood.

> **Self-control** in speech, mind and body: One should regulate habits of eating, sleeping, recreation and work by practising the yoga system. Avoiding criticism

> **A man should not hate any living creature. Let him be friendly and compassionate to all. He must free himself from the delusion of 'I' and 'mine'. He must accept pleasure and pain with equal tranquillity, he must be forgiving, ever contented, self-controlled ... A man's own duty, even if it seems imperfectly done, is better than work not naturally his own even if this is well performed.**
> *Bhagavad Gita*

and hurtful speech are important, and taking one's own responsibilities at home, at work and in caring for yourself.

Compassion in relation to nonviolence in speech, thoughts and actions. One should cultivate charity, humility and a favourable attitude towards other humans and living beings. Avoiding lust, anger and greed implies vegetarianism, morality and ethics, responsibility for one's own actions: this is connected to the law of karma.

Cleanliness: one should be clean internally and externally in relation to oneself, in thoughts and actions, keeping possessions neat and tidy.

For me, the purpose of these is to achieve fulfilment and grow exemplary human qualities – a foundation and prerequisite for spiritual success. This is the window into my Hindu world, and it's a far cry from the mystical, complex faith that many, including myself, once perceived.

Naina

Sanatan Dharma and the contemporary

Neera writes:

The most wonderful aspect of Hinduism as far as I am concerned is its openness and lack of rigidity. It is a belief system which encompasses the variety and plurality of human nature and experience. I therefore despair when I hear of 'Hindu militants' fighting with Muslims in Gujarat or British Hindus insisting that if Christians, Jews and Muslims have faith-based schools then Hindus should too. For me the joy of being a Hindu is that I do not have to convince myself of the supreme truth of my faith over any others; as Mahatma Gandhi said, 'Religions are different roads converging upon the same point. What does it matter that we take different roads so long as we reach the same goal?' Or to use a quote from the Bhagavad Gita, 'Whatsoever form any devotee desires to worship with faith – that (same) faith of his I make firm and unflinching.' I understand this as implying that it's not the name or rituals pertaining to a faith which are important, but how well people who profess to follow it really live by the ultimate rules of honesty, compassion and care which are common to all major faiths.

With respect to Hinduism there are many followers who are punctilious about observing fasts and festivals but without a spiritual involvement. Occasion has replaced devotion for some Hindus, or, as I find when speaking to young British Hindus, they participate to keep the culture alive, not from any spiritual sensibility at all. This is partially inevitable because very many British Hindus have Indian ancestry, but it also makes me sad that a rich and rewarding spiritual experience is being denied to people because they associate Hinduism with cultural identity and do not bother to explore the faith personally. Of course there is nothing wrong with celebration, story and ritual; it is when these means of expressing faith become enmeshed with social rules and family customs which young people find restrictive that they can become cynical about a faith which actually promotes acceptance and freedom.

Speaking as a woman, it was only when I read scriptures for myself and researched Hinduism that I realised that most of the sexist customs I had issue with emanated from social traditions, not from the religious heart of the tradition. My faith has also grown as I have learned to meditate and to reflect upon the glories of nature. Where I live at present, the view from my bedroom is of a beautiful valley; when the sun rises across the hills in the morning I have no need of a mandir or murtis, God is right there before me. This powerful attraction to God in the elements and sense of 'other' when I meditate is, I'm sure, far removed from most young people's understanding of what being a Hindu is all about, which is a pity, since it could open the door for otherwise closed hearts and minds. I believe it is vital in an age when young people

> Nonviolence is an active force of the highest order. It is soul force or the power of God within us. Imperfect man cannot grasp the whole of that Essence – he would not be able to bear its full blaze, but even an infinitesimal fraction of it, when it becomes active within us, can work wonders.
>
> *Mahatma Gandhi,* The Wisdom of Hinduism, *1932*

> Strong one, make me strong
> May all beings look on me with the eye of a friend
> May I look on all beings with the eye of a friend
> May we look on one another with the eye of a friend.
>
> *Yajur Veda 36:18*

> Sectarianism, bigotry and its horrible descendant fanaticism have long possessed this beautiful world with violence. He who loves all beings without distinction, he indeed is worshipping best his God.
>
> *Swami Vivekananda, Hindu reformer (1863–1902)*

are increasingly materialistic and insular that they have the inspiration and opportunity to get in touch with their spiritual being. Allowing them to access scripture from all faiths and interpret for themselves is essential to this, as is allowing space to ask questions and discover answers for themselves. This does not mean the main world faiths will provide the answers for all people and is not intended as a 'pick and choose' exercise. The point is that one cannot confirm the beliefs one professes to hold without having questioned them and compared them to alternative views. This is as true for being an atheist as it is for following a major faith. Indeed I personally believe it does not matter what label a person gives their religion (understanding 'religion' as the beliefs one lives by); what is important is spiritual awareness and a will to treat the world well.

To return to the question 'What is important to me about Hinduism?' I would summarise by saying that it is very important to me that Hinduism does not become a cultural label and that Hindus do not forget this insight: 'does it matter that we take different roads so long as we reach the same goal?'

Neera

Conclusion

Hinduism, as a very old religion, places great weight on living masters – gurus (male or female) – who, because they are established on a higher level of consciousness than the rest of us, are uniquely qualified to give spiritual guidance and show the practical relevance of the ancient scriptures for today. These are the sort of people who are looked up to as inspiring figures. Some recent (though not all still living) examples are Anandamayi Ma (f), Mata Amritanandamayi (f), Sathya Sai Baba (m), Shri Ramakrishna Paramahansa (m), Swami Vivekananda (m), AC Bhaktivedanta Swami (Prabhupad) (m), Swami Muktananda (m).

Authority lies in the scriptures and the guru, but also in the living experience of the individual seeker after truth, all of which act as checks. We hope we fall into the last category and, through the grace of our own traditions, we also hope that these articles will provide food for thought and be helpful to teachers approaching our religion.

Om Tatsat.

Helping teachers tackle my religion in the classroom
Guidance from inside the Jewish faith

In this article, **Anne Krisman** is the leading voice. She incorporates insights and extensive quotations from **Harvey Kurzfeld** and **Sandra Vincent** into the text, reflecting the diversities of the Jewish faith and the particular experiences of our three Jewish 'authentic voices'.

Anne Krisman is a special needs teacher in London.

Harvey Kurzfeld has retired from teaching in Cornwall.

Sandra Vincent is the head teacher of a primary school in Essex.

Representing Judaism

There are approximately 300,000 Jewish people in Britain, the second largest grouping after France. Many have expressed concerns about the future of the British Jewish community, with declining numbers of Jewish people who identify religiously, an ageing population and significant numbers of Jewish people marrying outside the faith. On the other hand, there is an enormous rise in the number of children attending Jewish schools. Half of Jewish children now attend Jewish schools and this number is set to rise. Some see this as extremely optimistic: 'For there is hope of a tree, if it is cut down, that it will sprout again' (Job 14:7).The rise of the right wing in Europe and tensions reflecting the conflict in the Middle East have had an impact on British Jewry, which has witnessed a disturbing rise in anti-Semitism. Organisations like the Three Faiths Forum, a grouping of Jews, Muslims and Christians, are working to create increased harmony and understanding between the faiths and to contribute to tikkun ha'olam (the healing and repair of the world).

Introduction: Diversity and unity

There is a diversity within Judaism that may not be communicated by textbooks. I have stayed with Orthodox friends in religious parts of Israel where every activity seems to carry a sense of holiness and spirituality. But that is just one strand of Judaism. Some of my friends see their Judaism as a political force, following the powerful sense of justice within the religion, fighting against racism, supporting refugees and campaigning for peace within the Middle East. For them, the essence of Judaism is conveyed in the teaching 'You shall not oppress a stranger; for you know the heart of a stranger, since you were strangers in the land of Egypt' (Exodus 23:9). There is a bond that unites us through our diversity, a shared history, shared stories, shared traditions, a respect for learning and a sense of enquiry.

My own Jewish identity comes very much from Eastern European Yiddish culture. I grew up in household where Jewish expression through the arts came before religious practice. My earliest memories are of listening to my mother's records of mournful songs of the shtetl (Yiddish for Jewish communities of the villages in Eastern Europe) and foot-tapping music from the klezmer tradition. Combined with that is my global identity. Despite being an Ashkenazi Jew, with my roots in Lithuania, Poland and Russia, I am drawn to the Sephardic culture of Spain and have a fascination with the period before the expulsion in 1492, the Golden Age, when Jews, Muslims and Christians lived together peacefully in Andalusia. My own work with children with special needs, highlighting how their suffering and difficulties often make them more able to understand challenging themes in RE, has its roots in my own experience of being Jewish and how I see the world.

> Let us magnify and let us sanctify the great name of God in the world which he created according to his will. May his kingdom come in your lifetime, and in your days, and in the lifetime of the family of Israel – quickly and speedily may it come, Amen
>
> *Jewish Kaddish Prayer*

> **To be a Jew is a destiny.**
> *Vicki Baum*

How do we communicate Judaism?

I took a group of 14-year-olds with special needs around an exhibition about Judaism, at a Jewish community centre. The exhibition was split into clear sections: festivals, kosher food, the synagogue and so on. The class found the experience a little cold. They were more interested in the young Jewish woman who showed us around (they all drew her as their 'favourite Jewish artefact' on their post-trip worksheet) and in the warmth shown to them by the elderly Jewish people in the day centre. They delighted in meeting the 90-year-olds who were painstakingly copying Chagall pictures in the art room. They loved spending their money on kosher sweets from the day centre's shop. They peered into the kosher kitchen and chatted with ladies having their nails done by helpers. These sparky encounters conveyed a powerful sense of community and the authentic spirit of Judaism.

These experiences have an analogy in the school trip around a synagogue. The silent synagogue, when the congregation are not there, does not communicate what Judaism is really about, its liveliness, its sense of togetherness. Looking at the Torah scrolls and spotting Star of David symbols is one thing, but it does not convey the way that the synagogue can be at the heart of the community, not just a place for prayer, but a base for religion school for the young, evening classes in Judaism for the adults, clubs for the elderly, a place where kosher meals on wheels are prepared for the needy and a place to socialise. The challenge for class teachers is to find a way of passing on this spirit of Judaism. It has to be done by meeting real Jewish people, and by using resources that convey the humanity of the religion (the BBC *Pathways of Belief* video on Shabbat has that authentic feeling). Using the internet to look for sites by the Jewish community for the Jewish community, for example www.totallyjewish.com can also communicate what real Jewish people think and feel.

Individuals as well as a community

Although the phrase 'Jewish community' feels comfortable to us, there is also a growing sense of people defining themselves individually. There are many who see themselves as 'cultural Jews', who identify through food, the arts, Jewish film and music much more than traditional religion. The more individual nature of society has affected us all. The tension between staying true to one's religion and following one's own choices and individuality is a strong theme in Judaism nowadays, whether it is to keep kosher, to marry within one's faith, to live within an area which has a synagogue nearby, or whether we send our children to Jewish schools. These challenges and personal boundaries may be interesting for older pupils to explore.

Many answers

Several RE teachers have asked me for the exact meaning of the objects on the seder table, as they find different textbooks say different things. This is no surprise to Jewish people; we say, three Jews four opinions! Much lively discussion is caused at seder nights by people using different Haggadot (books that show the order of service). Traditions depend on the cultural background of Jewish people. My Jewish friends from Calcutta make a special form of charoset, with date juice as well as chopped almonds and walnuts, called halek. As most Jewish festivals are home-based, often families develop their own customs – I remember a boyfriend's family nibbling matzos into circle shapes at the end of their seder to represent a rounded year ahead. As well as the traditional two seders, third seder meals have developed which explore the themes of liberation and freedom from oppression. There are third seders to acknowledge the achievements of Jewish women, for the environment, for vegetarians, for those with AIDS and HIV and to highlight the common experiences of the black and Jewish communities. This could provide a good activity to explore with pupils – what third seder could they plan, based on the Passover themes?

In that which we share, let us see the common prayer of humanity.
In that on which we differ, let us wonder at the freedom of mankind.
In our unity and our differences, let us know the uniqueness that is God.
May our courage match our convictions And our integrity match our hope.
May our faith in You bring us closer to each other.
May our meeting with past and present bring blessing for the future.
Amen

A Jewish prayer for inter-faith meetings

Respecting the Holocaust

In an assembly in my school, a teacher read out the touching poem which was found written on a wall of a cellar in Cologne where Jews had hidden during the Nazi occupation: 'I believe in the sun even when it's not shining. I believe in love even when not feeling it. I believe in God even when He is silent'. The assembly was not about the Holocaust – the message was to underline how the pupils should appreciate what they had. However, the reading created a stir around the hall and the hands kept going up ... who wrote it? How did they die? How old were they? The assembly was finished but the children's questions were just beginning. The answers did not seem to satisfy them. It underlined the power that the Holocaust has to disturb.

One Sikh boy once asked me why the Jewish people did not fight back against the Nazis, and the image of weakness and oppression may not fit with modern young people's images of themselves. My fear is that using the Holocaust to explore suffering may not open the door to exploring real life issues of Jewish bravery. A BBC Extreme Survival programme that showed an amazing story of how Jewish resistance fighters survived in the forests of Belarus, although inspiring to Jewish young people, may not fit into a scheme of work that is about the suffering Jew. However, resistance as a theme can lend itself to sharing stories of bravery and martyrdom from other faiths. It may also be more positive for the sense of identity and pride of the Jewish children who are studying RE in non-Jewish schools.

Rules

Judaism can be conveyed in the classroom as a collection of rules, about kashrut, Shabbat, prayer and so on. But rules without understanding the individual can seem heartless. My pupils love hearing stories about my Orthodox friends who tear the toilet roll into pieces ready for Shabbat (no tearing on Shabbat), my ex-boyfriend who had a special pair of jeans he only wore on Shabbat, and the people who take the battery out of their doorbell when Shabbat comes. These stories are about real people leading their lives. Too much emphasis on teaching about rules can also detract from the spirituality within Judaism – it is said, for example, that we gain an extra soul during Shabbat. Sandra Vincent writes here about her experiences:

'For Orthodox Jews like me, Shabbat is especially sweet. On Thursday evening, I spend lots of time cooking and preparing for Shabbat. On Friday, I arrive home before dark so I can light my Shabbat candles. I don't use any electricity, drive or cook on Shabbat. This makes it a very special and peaceful time for me – truly a day of rest. One weekend I went to stay with a family in Gateshead where there are some fine institutions for Jewish Higher Education. On the Friday evening after lighting my candles I was taken to the seminary where the girls study. There we prayed together to welcome Shabbat. In the service we always sing a special song welcoming Shabbat as if it were a bride. It has a lovely melody. On this occasion there were hundreds of girls and we women visitors singing in unison. The sound felt as if it was lifting the roof off the building! More than that, I felt it like an electrical charge through my body! We walked home in total silence, unable or unwilling to spoil the feelings we had. When the dinner was served, those of us who had heard the singing sat in silence – just nodding in response and smiling at others around the table. I can still remember how it felt and it's an inspiration to me to know how spiritual that feeling was.'

It is important to communicate the practical, lived nature of Judaism. The Chief Rabbi, Dr Jonathan Sacks, has said that Judaism is about faith lived and not faith thought. Shabbat is about living creation, and doing acts of loving kindness is about living redemption. This is shown in Sandra's experience:

> Never shall I forget that night The first night in the camp Which has turned my life into one long night. Seven times cursed and seven times sealed...
> *Elie Wiesel, Nobel Prize winner and Holocaust interpreter*

> Many causes of suffering are 'manufactured', rather than 'godufactured', but in my life I try to avoid oversimplifying such complex theological issues. We are told that the partner of suffering is joy.
> *Debbie Lewis, Jewish RE teacher*

> What is hateful to you, do not do to your fellow man.
> *Talmud: Shabbat 31a*

'I feel that the most important part of my religion is that there is no part of my life that is not affected by it! Judaism is a religion of practicality – we say, "Do and you will understand". For example, I thank God after every meal, snack or drink. I pray when I get up and before I sleep. I eat only kosher food. I try not to speak about others in any way that might harm them.'

Modern times

What effect has modernity had on traditional Judaism? How can technology help and hinder Judaism in practice? While Jewish style food has gone into mainstream culture, it creates dilemmas for Jewish people. I can now buy challah from Tesco, but it is not kosher. However, it is cheaper than kosher bread and is more convenient than going miles to a Jewish shop. The dependence on technology, automated burglar alarms, security lights, timers creates a pressure for families to create a peaceful Shabbat without dependence on them. The nature of today's society, with many of our pupils saying how stressed they are, can perhaps make Shabbat more relevant and understandable. Although traditional families are always shown in RE textbooks and the family nature of Judaism is accentuated, there are always going to be issues about people who are religious and yet not part of the conventional set-up. It is sometimes misleading to portray Shabbat mainly as a festival of family togetherness; plenty of people keep Shabbat when they are on their own. An interesting activity would be for pupils to design a set of 'travelling candlesticks' designed for someone who is backpacking around the world and still wants to celebrate Shabbat.

Two Jews – three opinions.

A famous proverbial reflection on Jewish diversity

Role models

Some concepts do not cross over easily between the faiths, and I suspect many Jewish people would find it difficult to name a contemporary Jewish role model who would equate with the significance of Martin Luther King or Mother Teresa for Christians. I am sure that many Jewish people would look within their community to members of their family, or teachers, as being central in their lives. Harvey Kurzfeld speaks about someone who has made a difference in the life of the Jewish community in Cornwall. It is the RE adviser, David Hampshire:

'David travelled the length and breadth of Cornwall, discovering the 'lost Jews' of Cornwall, none of whom knew the existence of each other. He and his wife Kathleen organised a get-together and the idea of forming a living, breathing branch of Judaism here in Cornwall took shape and our community was established. Kehillat Kernow, as we are now known, meets regularly for Shabbat and other festival services. Initially only David took services, but as others watched him we began to learn from his inspiring presentations. Now other members of the community run the services. David and his family continue to serve the community in many ways and we are often in awe of his store of Hebraic knowledge and expertise. Our successful community is a direct result of David's appearance in Cornwall. His influence has been so profound that were he and his family to move to another part of the country, the community would still continue to thrive and grow. That is the degree of confidence that we now have.'

Values

How far are Christian values actually similar to or the same as Jewish values? A sensitive issue for me is the way in which Jesus' Jewish heritage may not be highlighted in RE teaching. The fact that Jesus lived and died as a Jewish person needs to be accentuated. Jesus' teaching of 'love your neighbour as yourself' is clearly shaped from his Jewish heritage and our own ethical teachings – the rabbi Hillel, when asked to define the essence of Judaism, used to say, 'Whatever is hateful unto thee, do it not unto thy fellow. This is the whole law, the rest is commentary'.

I feel that misunderstandings can be caused when we fit other religions around the structure of Christianity: for example, when a scheme of work explores how Pesach 'fits into' Easter, or when the Creation story is described as 'the Christian Creation story'. When RE teachers explore the question 'why did Jesus tell stories?' some seem to present this as something unique to Jesus, whereas he was following a rabbinical tradition of telling stories.

Relationships with other faiths

Chief Rabbi Dr Jonathan Sacks tells a parable that shows the relationship between Judaism and people of other faiths. Two people have spent their lives carrying stones. One carries rocks, the other diamonds. Then they are asked to carry a consignment of emeralds. For the man who has spent his life transporting rocks, emeralds too are rocks. They are a burden and a weight. But to the man used to carrying diamonds, emeralds are also precious stones, different, but things of beauty and value. This has its analogy in our relationships with different civilisations and faiths. The person whose faith is precious will cherish the beliefs of others. He will see the beauty in each. The practice of Judaism should heighten our appreciation of the gifts of other cultures. The more we value what is in our own religion, the more we value the achievements of other 'languages of the spirit'.

> The Merciful demands that your servant be your equal. You should not eat white bread, and he black bread; you should not drink old wine, and he new wine; you should not sleep on a feather-bed and he on straw. Hence it was said, Whoever acquires a Hebrew slave acquires a master.
>
> *Talmud*

An activity on Judaism for 8-year-olds

Using two contrasting pieces of music, produce a movement piece in two scenes. One shows the stresses and pressures of everyday life, with everyone working very hard. The second scene, to calming music, shows the peacefulness of Shabbat. This idea can then be expressed through art – images can be collaged from magazines to show the working week, contrasted with symbolic images that show the peacefulness and rest of Shabbat.

> Pray for your enemies, that they may be holy and that all may be well with them. And should you think this is not serving God, rest assured that more than all prayers, this is indeed the service of God.
>
> *Talmudic instruction about prayer*

An activity on Judaism for 12-year-olds

Hillel, a Jewish teacher from the first century, was well known for his humanity and ethical teachings. He was once asked to teach the essence of Judaism while standing on one leg. He said, 'That which is hurtful to you, do not do to your fellow man.' Using Hillel's words 'If I am not for myself, then who is for me? But if I am only for myself, what am I? And if not now, when?', discuss what someone would be like if they:

a did not care about themselves;

b only cared about themselves;

c always thought about caring for others, but never put it into action.

An activity on Judaism for 15-year-olds

Children of Holocaust survivors living in Britain would like to construct a memorial for their families. Using the internet, investigate the design of some of the Holocaust memorials and museums which are around the world. Explore what themes and ideas are being explored through the design of the structures, including Rachel Whiteread's 'nameless library' for Vienna, the irregular shards of glass windows in Berlin, the Jewish ghetto architecture of the museum in Washington. Produce your own design. The survivors would like strong themes to be remembrance and also hope for a better world, where everyone is respected for their beliefs.

Lord, where shall I find you?
High and hidden is your place.
And where should I not find you?
The world is full of your glory.

I have sought your nearness
With all my heart I called you
And going out to meet you
I found you coming to meet me.

Judah Halevi

Helping teachers tackle my religion in the classroom
Guidance from inside the Muslim faith

Imran Mogra and Fatima Khan both teach RE in schools in Birmingham. The large and vibrant Muslim communities of Birmingham are the backdrop to their perspective on British Islam, and their insights are informed by the significant changes that the Muslim communities have been going through. The article asks early on some key questions about the presentation of Islam, and concludes with a 'wish list' for the development of how Islam is seen and understood through RE.

Imran Mogra is a primary teacher in Birmingham. He is RE subject leader at a large LEA primary school with a majority of Muslim pupils, and a member of PCfRE.

Fatima Khan is a secondary teacher of RE at an LEA school in Birmingham.

Islam: the religion

Islam is a practical religion based on surrendering to the will of God. It is a religion of service to God as the Creator, the Ruler, Sustainer and End of all existence. In addition, Islam is also attaining peace through the act of submission. Hence, it is a way of life and will incorporate all aspects of human endeavours. Al-Din is another term used for this.

Original inspiration

We believe Adam was a Muslim as he testified to the oneness of God. Therefore, Islam was there from the very start. The nature of humankind is forgetfulness and this oneness of God was forgotten. God in His mercy kept reminding His people through chosen messengers of this oneness of God. We see Islam as the original faith of Ibrahim, Musa and Isa. Therefore messengers recall people to that faith in the one God.

Muhammad ﷺ is the final messenger in this chain, which makes Islam the final religion. This is crucial for understanding Islam – it is based upon the oneness of God and not on any event, people or messenger.

Islam worldwide today

Modern-day followers of Islam constitute the second largest faith community in the world today (Christianity being the first): there are approximately 1 billion Muslim people, in every continent of the globe. Islam deserves to be known and represented correctly as an influential faith, which is increasingly having more and more relevance to both the religious and non-religious communities. In the UK today, there is great and interesting diversity of Muslims from all over the world.

Diversity within the faith: Muslims are not 'all the same'

Due to the fact that Muslims, like others, are from diverse regions and countries, their cultural differences will be reflected in their treatment of some aspects of Islam. In school, alertness to Islamic diversity is part of learning about Islam – for both staff and pupils.

For most Muslims, their primary identity is with Islam, not with a party, culture or sect within the religion, or with an ethnic group. However, not all Muslims look like the ones they see on television, films or in the newspapers. The questions that follow are intended to sensitise teachers to the issues we face in portraying Islam in Britain today.

> God is most powerful. He is not born, and does not give birth. He is the first and the last and he can destroy and bring back to life. He can do whatever he likes, whenever he likes. He is most kind and merciful, his kindness is greater than his anger. He is most forgiving and he sees and knows the feelings in our hearts.
>
> *Sumayya,*
> *11-year-old Muslim girl*

> ### Questions for those who teach Islam in RE about the presentation of the faith
> - Do Muslims have opportunities to speak for themselves?
> - Have you spoken to Muslim parents about what they would like to happen in school? A continuing dialogue is the best model here.
> - Does the subject matter selected for the curriculum reflect the self-understanding of Muslim people?
> - Which aspects of the curriculum content are ethnic or cultural in origin and which are from Islam?
> - How do the illustrations depict Muslims? (Inner-city corner shop? Butcher? Grocer?)
> - Is the material gender-balanced?
> - Who has written the material being used? Are Islamic writers or consultants evident?
> - Are Muslims projected as eccentric, or as ordinary British people?
> - Does the presentation of Muslims reflect their diverse social and ethnic origins?
> - What guidelines are followed in the teaching of terms from Islam? The QCA Glossary is a good starting point for teachers here.
> - How well is the community used as a resource? Could Islamic visitors be better used?
> - Is the school aware of the existence and role of Muslim charities, in the UK and abroad? Do these charities have a place in the curriculum? Are they recognised by pupils?
> - Has the school acknowledged and observed the relevance and spiritual importance of the Day of Arafat? Could the school provide an Eid dinner for Muslims?
> - Is there an awareness of the involvement of Muslims in national and local politics?

> *O mankind. We created you from a single pair of a male and a female and made you into nations and tribes, that you might know each other (not that you might despise each other). Verily, the most honoured among you in the sight of God is he who is the most righteous.'*
>
> Qur'an

The spiritual character of the religion

Islamic spirituality could be explained as the relationship that a Muslim has with God. In a world where God-fearing consciousness is being increasingly obliterated, it is worth taking note of how God – Allah – is perceived by Muslims.

The Holy Qur'an says: 'Allah is He, than whom there is no other god; Who knows (all things) both secret and open; He, Most gracious, Most Merciful. Allah is He than whom there is no other god; The Sovereign, the Holy One, The Source of Peace (and Perfection), The Guardian of Faith, The Preserver of Safety, The Exalted in might, The Irresistible, the justly Proud – Glory to Allah! (High is He) above partners they associate to Him. He is Allah the Creator, The Originator, The Fashioner – to him belong the most beautiful names: Whatever is in the heavens and on earth, doth declare His praise and Glory: And He is the Exalted in might, and the Wise' (Qur'an, 59:22–24).

Ultimately the Merciful Lord will judge the devotion by individuals to glorify Him, regardless of how strange or inadequate these might seem to other humans.

When God created the world He declared that His mercy will overcome His anger. Here lies the secret of those adverse and challenging times of life which seem, at times, incomprehensible and unfair.

Islamic laws are a manifestation of the Divine will. This finds expression in the Qur'an and the Sunnah. The law contained in both of these textual sources is the revealed law of Allah – the Shari'ah. However, the scope of Islamic law is wide. It comprises beliefs, rituals, civil and social transactions and ethics in the former, whereas some of the rituals and social transactions fall under the derivative category. It is crucial to recognise that in addition to the Divine law there is a huge intellectual tradition which guides the thinking of Muslims.

For Muslims, living in the British Isles (rather than in a Muslim majority country, or an Islamic state) does not mean that there is escape from the responsibility before God whose jurisdiction is over the world. Generally, Muslims have to bear in mind that Muslim law is personal in character and is therefore applicable to them wherever they may be. The law binds the individual; ultimately each one is responsible for his or her own actions.

Take the example of the requirements for prayer. Though the mosque is central to the British Muslim life for numerous activities, Salat (the five times of daily prayer) does not actually require a dedicated building. Prayer can be made from any pure place. This is an example of Islam's flexibility: prayer at various work places is not a problem.

The Islamic tradition offers spiritual and intellectual inspiration to followers today, for example through the constant invitation in the Qur'an to question, reflect and analyse the huge and beautiful creation. This may lead Muslim people to love science. The exemplary persons, as models for higher goals in life, who shoulder the trust and gift of God (may peace be upon them all) inspire a love of history.

The spiritual core of our faith is embodied in Ihsan (literally meaning to do a thing beautifully) and Tazkiya (purification). These two ideas lead to the cultivation of inner virtues, beautifying the soul, practising Shari'ah to the deepest level and conforming fully to the Sunnah and achieving the inner realities of faith.

It is not possible to speak of the spirituality of Islam without referring to the holy Qur'an: one British Muslim pupil put it like this: 'The Qur'an is a beautiful thing, the language and the style of writing in it is beautiful. It is extremely interesting as I discovered that every time you read it you find out something new. The rhythm of the words and the calligraphy are very beautiful.'

Islamic vision: ways in which we'd like to change the world

The vision of Islam is to inspire the love of God and the love of humans rather than the love of wealth or material possessions. Ideally, Muslims should stand up against all forms of oppression, injustice and evil in its various forms. By promoting the recognition and fulfilment of the duties that are necessary to the self, family, and society as a whole, Islam makes its contribution to human wellbeing.

Islam sees morality as an important aspect of religion and the essence of society. The religion joins the corporate life of people. The core mission of Islam is to encourage, develop and maintain the sense of good conduct and honour in the mind and heart of humankind. The Muslim community cherishes qualities such as mercy, forgiveness, modesty, charity, self-sacrifice, kindness, piety, justice and other high qualities of the Divine attributes. Islam calls upon its followers to beautify themselves with these virtues, and it's this which enables the possessor to become a perfect citizen and a spiritual luminary.

All deeds that are likely to degrade human dignity are to be avoided. Murder, alcohol, gambling and adultery are vices which are injurious to the healthy atmosphere of the society. Usury, interest and bribery are unlawful means of living for a Muslim.

> **Where Muslims are in a minority, especially in the West, they face a tension in their own lives. Whilst not wanting to put up a barrier to knowledge, they believe they must continue to live and think Islamically.**
> *Syed Ali Ashraf*

> **O Allah, I seek Your guidance through Your knowledge and ability, through Your power, and beg of Your infinite bounty; for You have power, and I have none, You know and I know not, and You are the knower of hidden things.**
> *Sunnah of the Prophet*

> **The Qur'an repeatedly teaches believers to ask for God's forgiveness and to be forgiving themselves. The Prophet was an extremely liberal and generous person.**
> *Syed Ali Ashraf*

> For the white to lord it over the black, the Arab over the non-Arab, the rich over the poor, the strong over the weak or men over women is out of place and wrong.
>
> *Hadith of Ibn Majah*

> People of one faith who have not surveyed other faiths cannot claim to have a monopoly of truth for they do not know what the other faith says. Islam does not allow mission work through coercion, but only by reasoning with others in a better way (Qur'an 16:125). It cannot rubbish Judaism or Christianity for it believes in the same God and all the prophets of Judaism and Christianity. It allows freedom of religion by saying that there is no compulsion in religion (Qur'an 2:256) and allows religious pluralism by wishing to others their faiths, and to Muslims their faith. (Qur'an 109:6).
>
> *Asaf Hussain, Islamic Rights Organisation*

The aim of this ethical vision of Islam is to improve life in this world and to come to salvation in the Hereafter, the next life.

The fact should not be ignored that religion is the fountainhead of morality; it is the primary cause of existence and essence of life. Without religion, would not life be meaningless? In moral terms, religion is the bona fide incentive towards that which is good and a valid deterrent that keeps a person away from that which is bad. The study of Islam in RE lessons can provide the impetus to kindle a flame in pupils so that they may 'adorn themselves' with virtues. This is part of what it means to 'learn from Islam'.

Islam envisages a world in which individuals mutually forbid one another from evil and encourage good actions. If learners in school come to see that Islam is a living religion rather than just a philosophical thought or an intellectual concept in a book, then a challenge emerges: Islam is in fact an all-encompassing way of life: a creed, practice, a stream of consciousness, a communal attitude, a moral principle providing a system of life which reinvigorates in human beings a new life direction, a new pattern, a new goal and a new meaning.

Human life in Islam

Between God and humans – there is everything and nothing. There is nothing between a human and Allah, as God declares that He is closer to us than our own jugular vein and He is there wherever we are (50:16). Yet people erect barriers between the self and Allah in the form of bad actions, hence God would seem to be at a distance. The start of the never-ending life follows death. This is not something to be feared but something to look forward to. In Islam, death is a bridge to Allah.

Islam among the world's religions

The Qur'an states that all problems of life and afterlife that relate to people are implicitly or explicitly dealt with in Islam: '…We have revealed unto thee the Book, as an exposition of everything' (16:89). This comprehensive guidance has been planned under the name of Al-Islam on the basis of faith in the One God and all that it implies.

This implies Islamic respect for others. The Qur'an says: 'We have created you out of different nations and tribes so that you can recognise one another…' (16:89). The maintenance of goodwill towards others is encouraged in Islam. Muslims have a duty of respect, to treat all human beings according to their fundamental rights as fellow creatures – regardless of differences of gender, race or colour. The Qur'an requires people to be respected in, for example, their rights of property, life and honour. Indeed as a consequence of this status of equality, the rights of freedom and the right to fraternise with others follow – except when these are superseded by a just moral cause.

A Muslim recognising one Creator sees the creation and humanity in particular as one. All beings are equally Allah's creation. External difference, whatever form it may take, is a wonderful sign of the beauty of God. These outward differences do not constitute a raison d'être for looking either up or down to another individual. The only criterion acknowledged by Islam is that of moral and spiritual qualities.

In relation to others' faiths, we believe in co-operation in goodness with non-Muslims and being sympathetic with them in rescuing people from moral evils and spiritual decay. Co-operation in transgression and sin is prohibited. Social interaction and kindness is endorsed. However, with active enemies firmness is enjoined. The attitude of being prepared for making peace and maintaining peace in the interest of human good is promoted. Honouring non-Muslim parents is required from us as Muslims.

Islam: a living faith

Many young people are thriving and enjoying the vitality of Islam in Britain, with a large range of associations and youth movements to choose from. They are being catered for by various organisations. Their programmes are immensely varied, ranging from annual conferences and summer camps to groups interested in specific issues running on a monthly or weekly basis. Sometimes daily gatherings ensure that the spiritual, intellectual, social and moral thirst of our next generation is being quenched from the fountains of Muslim knowledge and wisdom. Many major cities host Islamic radio programmes especially during Ramadan. We find this commitment most encouraging: many Muslim youngsters in Britain have a strong sense of purpose. Some of these assemblies encourage discussions, debates and learning about traditional Islam and its relation to modern scientific and technological knowledge. Many current concerns are dealt with by the Muslim press with a variety of English language magazines, newspapers, and periodical leaflets which accommodate all viewpoints. The World Wide Web is fully utilised for learning and sharing of ideas. An increasing trend in Islam in Britain is the commitment towards spiritual uplift and reformation.

Islam, it seems, is providing answers of enduring validity to some of these young people educated in modern thought.

Some challenges for Muslims in the UK

British Islam faces challenges today: here are some examples. A basic tenet of Muslim life is to perform charitable actions. Communal organisations serve to meet specific projects where the local statutory welfare provisions are insufficient for Muslim needs. These organisations need to form partnerships to create orphanages, homes for elderly people, help for lone-parent families and runaway teenagers in an environment that is contributing to Muslim needs and identities. There are issues about divorce and assisted marriages.

An exploration of the history and morality of extremism in all its guises, whether in religious or non-religious forms, is another challenge. The aim of this would be to demonstrate the origins of intolerance and religiously inspired violence and cause students to think critically about how these ideas affect Islam in an age of increasing globalisation and egalitarianism.

We are facing the challenge of promoting greater understanding within Islam of non-Muslim culture in order to provide an appreciation of how Islam is popularly perceived by the outside world. We need to help young people to distinguish true values, whether from the 'west' or the 'east', and to see clearly how the media can communicate ideology very subtly. Hats and hijabs can be problematic, mainly due to ignorance in schools and workplaces. Education, employment practice and media have been highlighted as areas where religious discrimination is most likely against Muslims. There is a moral case for extending the protection of the blasphemy law to include Islam and other religions alongside Christianity.

Some young Muslims feel alienated and are dissatisfied with society as a whole. This raises serious and challenging questions: What are the causes of split identities in some Muslims? What is contributing toward some Muslims becoming dysfunctional in society? Where else in society – as well as in RE lessons – are young people motivated to work for the betterment of the society as a whole? In terms of intra-faith unity, to what extent has the public purse resourced Muslim endeavours and initiatives?

The challenge of the role of popular culture in forming young people's identity is testing. Fair representation should enable the position of any religion to be stated clearly, with the aim of educating those within and beyond that faith. Currently, we are far from this in Britain. For example, if due to the influence of popular culture a

> Humankind, especially the marginalised and oppressed, need each other to confront the many dangers and challenges of liberation. Let us hope that because of (and not despite) our different creeds and worldviews we are going to walk this road side by side.
>
> *Farid Esack, South African contemporary Islamic theologian*

> Islamic charities like Muslim Aid, the Red Crescent and Islamic Relief are excellent starting points for learning Islamic ethics.

> No one of you is a believer until he loves for his brother what he loves for himself.
>
> *Forty Hadith of an-Nawawi, 13*

> Spend out of love for Him, for your family, for orphans, for the refugee, for those who have need.
>
> *Qur'an, Surah 2:17*

> There are an estimated 100 Muslim schools in the UK, of which five are government-funded. Many Muslims would like a holistic education for their children – one that is not only academic and scientific but also especially spiritual. They would rather, for example, have the water cycle taught as God's wonderful mechanism for sustaining life as well as explained scientifically.
>
> *Ibrahim Mogra, Principal of a Leicester Madrasah*

Muslim child expresses a belief in reincarnation, then it should be the educational role of the teacher to state the authentic position of Islam on the question of life after death.

Some contributions to UK society from the faith

Muslims, along with people of other beliefs, make considerable and wide-ranging contributions to UK society. From public services to sport and voluntary action, and from heart specialists to hospital porters, British Muslims 'do their part' for the society as a whole. There is a thriving Muslim business community. The architectural landscape has been changed with the building of magnificent mosques in most major cities.

A question is frequently put into the public domain about whether Britain is a Christian nation. It raises interesting questions of religion and identity for Islam in the UK. A teacher in RE might raise questions like these: Are British people Christians? What about British Muslims? Could the electorate choose a Muslim prime minister? If so, how would she or he take her oath?

Teachers may need to think more deeply about these questions: if Christianity is the historical hegemonic religious paradigm in the British context, what does that mean for Britain's 1.5 million Muslims? In an increasingly secular state, which in some ways has a distinctive relationship with an established church, how do we create space for the meeting between religions? In publicly funded schools, are Christian confessional values as strange for the school as Islamic values? Are there shared values? Is it possible to speak about formal or institutional Christian and Islamic values?

We hope that good representation of Islam in school can contribute to the young lives of thinking, believing and practising Muslims. For a healthy and happy life, young Muslims need to develop faith and taqwa (realisation of God through the guidance of knowing right from wrong). If the school undermines this, or fails to assist it, then the young person may be stuck living solely for the material things of this world. We see this as a disservice to the child.

Presenting Islam in school RE

Many British Muslim adults remember being taught simple Islam which consisted of the five pillars, the 'do's and the don'ts' and of course the festivals. Good RE might aspire to go beyond this, so that children and young people learn more, and learn to reflect more deeply on the relevance and meaning of Islam as a way of life in RE lessons. We hope RE might lead young people to be confident in addressing the challenge of Islamophobia in society.

Some good developments from the current situation in RE and in school generally might include:

- Some young British Muslims – and members of the older generation – look with suspicion or ill feeling on the wider British society. RE can make a difference here. It is time for the distinctions between faiths to be given an equal space with the promotion of human equality and the incorporation into teaching of the morals and virtues common to all faiths.

- Bringing Islam into the school, rather than implicitly telling Muslim pupils to 'leave it at home' is good. We heard someone say in a staff room, in the context of separate collective worship, 'Why don't these children go to the mosque if they want to learn and worship Islam?' We think the school would be the poorer for such a separation.

- In a learning situation, the relation between one's self-image and self-esteem and the will to learn is well-known. In the places where Muslim children are essentially a minority community, it is most important and a key prerequisite that these

> Prophet Muhammad, messenger of God, taught me these things: I have learned that to respect another human being regardless of his religion will make me a better person.
>
> *Haimi, 12-year-old Muslim boy*

children attending schools have good self-esteem through the acceptance and recognition of their faith. It cannot be assumed that self-esteem will automatically be instilled in these children. The question therefore is: what active measures can the school take to ensure that Muslim children have good self-esteem, especially in the light of very negative media representations of Islam? The RE lesson's approach to Islam can contribute towards this.

- Acknowledging the contribution of Islam in other curriculum areas, not only in RE, is important. Islamic science, art and design technology would be good starting points.

- Showing increasing sensitivity to Islamic ways of life. One example is with regard to pigs. Recently a class with a majority of Muslim children visited a farm. To the surprise of some teachers, many Muslim children had gone and spent some time observing the pigs. It was the teacher, a non-Muslim, who first had enough of the foul smell! While all Muslims must not eat anything derived from the pig, practice varies with regard to portrayal of the animal. Any role-play of pigs is best avoided, being likely to hinder the lesson objective.

- A proper presentation of Islam in a non-Muslim environment must have a suitable emphasis on the 'rationale' of Islam and its 'practice' (ritual or cultural). Pupils must see the dynamism and personal spiritual nature of the Muslim experience.

- Schools need actively to seek ways to recognise the Muslim way of life and its implications for everyday school activities. Halal and Haram are not only about food and drink. RE lessons can explore the questions of this concept in relation to other activities both in and out of school.

- Is Islam studied from a non-Eurocentric perspective as a religion of more than 1 billion people or are the displays typically of the 'five pillars perspective', seeing the faith as easily summed up by ritual practice? It needs to be made clear that Islam in fact is a liberating religion for the whole of humanity.

- By religion and faith, Muslims belong to Islam. They are neither Asians nor Turks, Africans or Chinese, but spiritually Muslims. However, aspects of their ethnic culture need to be respected and this would include giving consideration to them in matters such as uniform, PSHE or sex education.

- There is the question of who Muslims are. Identity categories are often confused. Reports frequently refer to pupils as Pakistani, Bangladeshi and Turkish. Many of these pupils have never visited these countries and many might not be speaking their own language. Is their Britishness recognised? Their language, their education, their place, their work and their life are oriented around the major features of Britishness yet this is ignored. The question to be addressed is: what is the position of Muslims in school? Who are they in a typical mainstream UK school?

- Even if there are Muslim pupils in a class they may not all have a full understanding of the rationale of some of the practices of Islam. It would be unfair to expect them to talk about, for example, Ramadan and its complexities. It is education-ally inappropriate for a teacher to say to a Muslim pupil reluctant to speak to the whole class 'if you don't know why you are fasting, then why are you fasting?' (a recent example reported by a Muslim child). A good strategy would provide some initial explanations and be followed by pupils' invited contributions and experi-ences.

- Where there are Muslim pupils in school, the educational, spiritual and social benefits of arranging a place for Islamic prayer are immense.

- RE's portrayal of Islam needs authentic voices from the inside. Have you had in your school someone who performed Hajj 30 years ago and visited the holy lands again this year? Could they share the experience and relate the changes?

> In RE lessons, you get to know a lot about other religions and it helps you understand the followers better. What I like about RE is that it is open-minded and it condemns no one. RE is modern and deals with issues today and things that happen and some of us go through.
>
> *13-year-old Muslim girl*

> In my RE lessons I have learned to become more broad-minded, to accept other peoples beliefs and faiths and to not let race or religion come in the way of what you see in an individual. What I like about my RE lessons is that my opinion is heard and I can find out what my fellow students' opinions are.
>
> *14-year-old Muslim girl*

The important thing to aim for is to make sure that pupils attending mainstream schools feel confident about being Muslims and do not harbour any inferiority complex because they are Muslims. All this is about inclusion. It isn't reasonable to have the pupils 'in' and their religio-cultural elements 'out'. Does confidence not emanate from who you are and how comfortable you are with your identity?

We are personally concerned that even in schools with a majority of Muslim pupils, some pupils may still view a school as a 'white man's school'. This is an issue for the school, for the society and for the home. Questions of belonging and a sense of ownership arise here: are we, as RE teachers, content to be 'doing something', or should we be ambitious to do more?

There are many historical distortions and current misconceptions about Islam and educators need to raise awareness so that they do not perpetuate and reinforce them, thereby giving offence to Islam and some Muslims.

All the same? Distinctive Islam

One of the most common practices that we have witnessed is the declaration that 'we are all the same' especially in relation to RE. What does this mean precisely? Where is similarity directed? Is it in terms of religion, humanity, in celebrating festivals or what? Good RE draws attention to what is similar between religions, and what is distinctive.

One example is that in order to emphasise similarity many pupils are taught that stories from the Qur'an are the same as those in the Christian Bible and the Jewish sacred writings. This is usually done in good faith, but in fact, even though some of the characters are the same, there are differences in the fundamental beliefs about them and their roles, in the interpretation of their events and in the morals that are derived from them. Who are prophets? Which ones are prophets in Christianity or Judaism and which ones in Islam? When using stories from the Qur'an it is useful to use writings from within the faith with sensitivity to all other pupils as well.

Although some Muslim pupils will participate in Nativity plays, or take acting parts in stories of Hindu deities, when told to do so by teachers, this will place parents in a dilemma of whether or not to offend the teacher or the school's head by raising an objection. There have been occasions when some Muslim pupils burst into tears after realising what they had actually participated in, through carelessly planned drama.

How Islam might challenge school pupils today

A young British Muslim related the experience of 'doing Islam' in school like this: 'At school, I was taught Islam in comparison to other religions and unfortunately, as we lived in an area where there was no mosque or Muslims, this was the first time I was taught anything at a "serious level" about my religion other than what my parents had taught me. So I believed it would be very important to ensure that the basics of Islam were introduced thoroughly, not only for many Muslim children, but also bearing in mind the content is being delivered to non-Muslims as well.'

In Islam, education matters greatly, and a true religious upbringing is crucial. The goal is development of a comprehensive Muslim personality which staunchly believes in that which is good, strives hard in promoting its cause, enjoins that which is right and forbids that which is evil, stands firm in facing oppression and injustices, and strives hard to translate religious principles into real practice.

Teaching Islam in school RE has a contribution to make to learning for all pupils. Muslim pupils, and non-Muslims living in plural communities, and those who are part of local communities where there are few or no Muslims can all learn much from

> The Qur'an tells Muslims to accept all previous prophets as their own, never to criticise any previous prophet, or use abusive terms against even the gods and goddesses of other religions (6:108), to invite others to Islam [submission to the divine] with beautiful speech and with wisdom and good admonition (16:125), and never to use compulsion (2:256).
>
> *Syed Ali Ashraf*

RE's study of Islam. Children and young people in schools may find it challenging to see the open position of Islam. It might be interesting for some to discover what appeals to Muslims from Islam. Through the study of Islam, pupils' incorrect perceptions and stereotypical views should be challenged, so that they become more enlightened and better informed. If the teaching enables them to see the importance of religion in the lives of Muslims and consider what it is that attracts people to this faith despite so much adverse publicity and apparent hostility, then their learning has a social purpose. Studying Islam should offer mainstream pupils the opportunity to consider the growth of Islam in Britain and how it is now a part of the fabric of religion in the United Kingdom.

Classroom activities

The next two pages provide some practical examples of activities which take the ideas in the article about teaching Islam in to the classroom. The first page is for primary pupils, the second for secondary.

It is important that Muslim organisations and scholars in this country work in conjunction with other educationalists to plan and produce enough authentic material, including teachers' guides which will not have the defects [of perpetuating stereotypes, or flaws in implication or information].
As most of the teachers teaching RE are non-Muslim, this lack of adequate authentic material is a serious drawback.

Islamic Academy,
University of Cambridge

Moon and star: symbols to light and guide

One explanation of the Islamic symbol of a moon and star is that Islam is like the stars – it guides your way – and like the moon – it lights your path. Get pupils to look at examples of the Islamic symbol (on flags, mosques, from books, as a car sticker, and so on). Get them to make a beautiful one themselves. Talk about lighting and guiding as symbols. Ask pupils to make a symbol for the thing that guides them and the thing that lights their path. This is a simple example of learning from religion.

In what ways are places to worship important?
Islamic materials for 7–9s

- How can you show respect for a holy place? Prepare pupils for a visit to a mosque (you could use a virtual visit). Discuss appropriate behaviour and respect for a place of worship. Pupils could work out a list of questions, prior to the visit, about the uses of the building. Arrange for a member of the mosque's community to answer the questions. During the visit, emphasis should be placed on allowing the pupils to focus on the atmosphere in the mosque, and to reflect on their feelings, as well as learning about the purposes and activities of the place of worship – they might sit quietly and listen to a short Quranic recitation, or a story of the Prophet.

- What do Muslims say about their holy places? Arrange in advance with the community to provide a hands on experience for the pupils, or organise this in the classroom. For example, pupils taste some Eid sweets, eat dates (used to break the fast in Ramadan), hear music, feel the carvings on a Qur'an stand, listen to the prayer call, look at the tiles, ornamentation and calligraphy used to decorate the mosque or some manuscripts, or examine how wudu (washing) contributes to the atmosphere of prayer. Multisensory RE is powerful learning.

- What atmosphere do mosques have? Pupils could make a booklet explaining what they have learned following their visit and what they would like to find out more about. They should be encouraged to describe the atmosphere in the mosque, and to remember how they felt. This can link to 'adjectives' work in literacy, or simple poetry. Why do they think that Muslims go to mosque? In what ways is a mosque like a library, or a community centre, or a home? And how is it different? Why do Muslims sometimes speak of the mosque as the 'house of prayer' or the 'place of prostration'?

- What places have an atmosphere for me? Talk about atmospheres of peace, cleanness, being 'all together' familiar to the children: are they similar to or different from these feelings at the mosque? What is the atmosphere of worship? Prayer?

- Being kind to those who are different: what do Muslims do to make visitors welcome at the mosque? How can a town, a school or a class be welcoming, kind or respectful to those who are different?

Islam: it means 'peace'.

These activities aim to help any pupils to think for themselves, open-mindedly, about peace in Islam and in the world. What do British Muslim teenagers have to say about Islam and peace? We asked some of them. Here are nine thoughtful replies:

At Ramadan time, fasting, I felt peace because I felt how the poor people suffer.
Foiza (15)

Islam gives me peace in many ways: Praying five times a day, reading from the Qur'an, giving zakah, fasting during the month of Ramadan, going to Hajj, to complete pilgrimage.
Nazma (16)

I felt the peace of Islam when I spent the whole night reading the Qur'an (the Night of Power). I think it is a very powerful night for all Muslims.
Mina (16)

I always feel peace when my family pays their zakah. It feels like we have given back to Allah what really belongs to Him. It isn't much really and it is used to do so much good.
Fatema (15)

Islam gives you peace though prayer. Prayer takes everything off your mind as you concentrate on Allah alone.
Anon (15)

I felt the peace of Islam when I started to read the Qur'an and started to pray. But my very first feeling of peace was when I saw my Dad praying and that peace is still in me and will stay there forever.
Suhela (16)

Although some Muslims use Islam to justify their actions, they cannot when they do something that is against Islam. Many people do this and Islam is perceived as a violent, unjust religion. But Islam is peace.
Tahera (16)

I felt the peace of Islam when I went on Hajj, the Muslim pilgrimage. The most amazing sight ever! You see the Ka'aba on the calendar every day but seeing it directly was just amazing, breathtaking. The unity of Muslims makes you feel on top of the world when all the barriers of language, colour and nationality are disregarded.
Asma (16)

I get peace from al-Fatiha [the opening surah of the Qur'an]. Allah is merciful and everlasting. His love is for everyone, whether you are a Muslim, Christian or Hindu, you are all part of Allah. Allah loves all His people, no matter how many sins they have made. Allah loves everyone equally.
Naeema (16)

Here are some tasks for pupils to talk about and think through, using the quotations from Hadith and from our young Muslim respondents:

- Starter: begin a lesson by asking pupils to note down, anonymously, five things that they think contribute to peace. Get half the class to note things to do with world peace, and half to do inner peace, 'peace within'.
- Read aloud and discuss each of the quotations in pairs, groups or circle time.
- Ask pupils to highlight in colour: what is interesting? What is surprising? What don't you understand? What is about inner peace? What is about world peace? Pair to discuss.
- Ask pupils to explain how each of the actions of the Five Pillars of Islam might contribute to personal peace and to community peace.
- Explain what each of the three Hadith means in terms of peace.
- Relate the ideas of these young Muslims to their own ideas of peace: ask pupils what their ideas for the beginning of the lesson, and the Muslim ideas have in common.
- Set a writing task about 'What makes for peace?' You could use the old formula of a recipe, or invite pairs of pupils to make proposals to the UN, or any task between these two!

Hadith about peace
Muslims understand the world and its problems in the light of Hadith of the Prophet Muhammad ﷺ. Here are three Hadith to think about:

In the name of One in whose Hand is my soul, you will not enter Heaven till you believe, and you will not believe till you love one another. Shall I tell you what will lead you to love one another? Spread peace among yourselves.

Islam means that you should testify that there is no God but Allah and that Muhammad is the Messenger of Allah, that you should observe the prayer, pay the zakah, fast during Ramadan, and make the pilgrimage to the Ka'aba if you have the means to go.
Muslim Hadith 1.001

Whoever kills a person from the dhimmi (Non-Muslim at the time of the Muslim State) is not going to smell the fragrance of Heaven; a scent that one can smell a distance of 70 years from Heaven.
Bukhari Hadith

Take two well scrubbed warring parties, and mix them slowly together with a pinch of tolerance, half a kilo of well sieved respect, and a spoonful of listening. Marinate overnight in a mixture of integrity and sensitivity, and cook slowly for at least 2 hours – in a moderate oven. Serve with a tossed salad of leaves from the tree of peace, and plenty of bread and butter.

Helping teachers tackle my religion in the classroom:
Guidance from inside the Sikh faith

This article has been written in its current form by Surinder Lall. She is a primary school teacher and RE co-ordinator from London, and used a Farmington Fellowship period of study leave to investigate the teaching of Sikhism among young children, with a particular emphasis on the concept of God. It is the product of collaborative work and thinking with Sundeep Gill; she is a primary school teacher from London as well.

> There is one God, eternal truth is his name, maker of all things. Fearing nothing and at enmity with nothing, timeless is his image, not begotten, being of his own being, by the grace of the guru made known to humanity.
>
> *Translation of the opening lines of the Japji*

> Some bathe at Hindu holy places, some go to perform the Hajj. Some engage in puja, some bow their heads in prayer. Some study Vedas, some read the Bible or Qur'an...
> But whoever does the will of God, to him all things are revealed.
>
> *Guru Arjan*

Nanak Naam chardi kala tere bhane sarbat da bhala
(*Translation:* In the name of God, do something for somebody else)

This thought has become part of my life, something that I try to live every day with my family and all those I meet. This adult understanding of my Sikh faith is built on the foundations my parents laid. In their way of bringing us up, there was no sense of Sikhism as a category, only a sense of 'this is our way of life'. We lived, worked and celebrated with those around us, sharing food and festivals and never being taught to see ourselves as separate. We were more exposed to the spirit of our faith than to the formalities of organised religion, the 'dos and don'ts' that would have made us feel different. It is the spirit which is the dialogue with God, not the formality, as any child would tell you. This generous, open and diverse spirit of Sikhism is what I would love to see presented as the truth of Sikhism taught in the classroom, rather than concentrating on formalities.

Origins: Guru Nanak

The original inspiration of Sikhism came from the vision and understanding of Guru Nanak in the late fifteenth century. He taught within the Indian Sant tradition, emphasising personal experience of God the Creator, the only reality, who is to be worshipped by meditation on his Name. Born a Hindu, Nanak spent his time with companions of different faith backgrounds, and you can imagine him involved in sharing ideas, telling stories and singing – just look at the miniatures of Guru Nanak with Bhai Mardana and Bhai Bala and you can almost hear him challenging preconceptions and opening their eyes to the wonder of God. He must have held teaching sessions where his questions challenged his hearers and opened the door for them to move further along their own spiritual path. Isn't that what we want as teachers in our RE lessons? Or are we happy to let pupils believe that 'All Sikhs ... all Hindus ... all Christians ... all Muslims ...' believe and practise the same?

Essentially Guru Nanak rejected caste and ritual in all traditions.

To Hindus he said:

'Let contentment be thine earrings
Modesty thy begging bowl,
Smear thy body with the ashes of meditation.'

To Muslims he said:

'Let compassion be thy mosque,
Let faith be thy prayer mat,
Let honest living be thy Qur'an ...
Let piety be the fast thou keepest.'

His vision of religion was one of living a truthful, faith-filled life, focused on God, but in the everyday world. As a community grew around him, there began to develop

characteristics of Sikh practice still recognisable today. It was a family-centred way of life, with no separate 'higher order' of celibates or priestly group. Faith was focused through the Guru (a community leader as well as a teacher), and expressed by personal meditation, by communal meditation in the form of singing of kirtan (poetry in praise of God taken from the Guru's writings), and by service to the community.

Guru Nanak constantly insisted that the external was of no value on its own, saying that stating belief in a particular faith or category had no meaning. The only true believers were those who were willing to learn about God; the word 'Sikh' comes from the verb 'to learn', so the followers of Guru Nanak were nicknamed 'learners'. All 'learners' were equal in Guru Nanak's eyes, and when he began to gather the devotional writings which later formed the basis of the Sikh scriptures, he included not only his own but the writings of Hindus and Muslims as well, making the Guru Granth Sahib unique among holy books.

> Words do not a saint or sinner make. Action alone is written in the book of fate.
> *Guru Nanak*

The ten Gurus and the living Guru Granth Sahib

The Gurus who followed Nanak developed his teachings, some of them becoming more formalised but still retaining the sense of equality and accessibility to all, such as the Langar (the Guru's free kitchen). The Sikh community, initially a rather loosely connected group, was forced into more visible recognition by external forces, especially the pressure of the Moghal invaders who were trying to impose their religion as a means of subduing the population.

The tenth Guru, Guru Gobind Singh, was under even more external pressure than previous Gurus. The war with the Moghals was at its height and within the Sikh community there were divisions often based on ancient Hindu caste divisions. The Guru had to protect the future of his Sikhs, to ensure that they could follow their way of life, but at the same time he needed to unravel the complications of the caste system. So the Khalsa was formed, a group of soldier-saints easy to recognise, equal in status, committed to their beliefs and ready to fight and die to protect their community. In the Sikh tradition, living a true life included seeking justice as an essential outcome of the worship of God, although Guru Gobind Singh made it very clear to his followers that external observance of the rules of the Khalsa was nothing without the true faith in the heart.

> In Sikhism we believe there are three different sources of the gift of truth. The first is God, and God gives the truth directly to people who are holy and enlightened – only the pure ones, not all of us. The second source is the Guru Granth Sahib, that can give truth through the teachings of the gurus. The third source is the Sadhsangat, the congregation.
> *Virpal Kaur*

The presentation of Sikh unity and diversity

Textbooks necessarily present information very simply, and it is easy to pick up the idea that the development of Sikhism from the time of Guru Nanak to the formation of the Khalsa was a seamless whole, leaving a single form of Sikhism practised by all. However, while many Sikhs are wholeheartedly committed to the ideals of the Khalsa, there is also a range of folk and traditional practices, caste-based devotions and a number of sects within Sikhism which developed from the time of Guru Nanak onwards. (For detail on these, see *The Evolution of a Sikh Community in Britain* by Kalsi, Sewa and Sing, University of Leeds, 1992, or *Britain's Sikhs* by Eleanor Nesbitt.) Some of those who belong to these diverse groups 'look like' Sikhs as the textbooks present Sikhs, and some do not. Teachers need to be alert to the possibility of Sikhism being present in their classrooms in many different forms, not all corresponding to official definitions. When you look at the pupils sitting in your class you may recognise the boy with the turban and kera as a Sikh, but do you equally recognise others, for example the boy with the Nike tick cut into the back of his short hair, who may be wearing a kera or not? One 12-year-old boy said, 'Most people think I'm a Hindu because they see I haven't got a turban. I always have to constantly say, "No, I'm a Sikh!"'

Sikhism's heartland is the Punjab, but from the nineteenth century Sikh families were among those who emigrated to find new opportunities. There are particularly large

> I like to live according to what my religion says. When Guru Nanak met God, he came back and preached the teachings of God. I would like to live by what he said, although it can be hard sometimes!
>
> *Mandeep,*
> *15-year-old Sikh girl*

> A gurdwara, literally 'the guru's door' is a rendezvous chosen by the guru or by Sikhs for meeting and speaking about God and for public worship. It is a place of meditation, divine knowledge, bliss and tranquillity.
>
> *G Singh Sidhu, the Sikh*
> *Missionary Society*

> I think to pray is a good thing to get on the right side of God. It refreshes your mind, tells you to respect others, basically takes you on to the right paths. And makes you to be proud of what you are, not of what others say.
>
> *15-year-old Sikh girl*

communities in Canada, America and Great Britain. Immigration to Britain began in the 1960s and has included Sikhs from all the diverse groups referred to above. These groups have now built community centres and gurdwaras, which exhibit differences of practice and thought. This process has not stopped, and the Sikh community from Afghanistan who are the most recently arrived are beginning to set up their own centres now.

Know your gurdwara

It is helpful for teachers to get to know the gurdwaras in their local community so that they know where their pupils come from. All gurdwaras welcome non-Sikh visitors and would particularly welcome interest shown by teachers. Don't be afraid to ask questions or be worried if you get a range of different answers. Try to get to know a few families and to hear about Sikhism as it is lived.

What all gurdwaras and Sikh homes have in common is the welcome that greets the visitor. If you visit a gurdwara you may be assailed by people, from small children to grannies, anxious to make you feel at home and to explain and show you whatever you ask. Be prepared to eat and drink even if what you are offered seems strange to you. You will be invited to eat in the langar, where everyone, male and female, Sikh and non-Sikh, rich and poor, is absolutely equal in God's house. You will be offered prasad. This cooked semolina sweet is made from food donated by the community and is shared after prayer or when you visit the gurdwara as an individual. It cannot be equated to the Christian Eucharist, but it is something to be treated respectfully, never to be thrown away or dropped on the floor. To receive prasad shows that you are not distancing yourself by rank or caste but that you are willing to share what the Guru's community is offering, as you would share in the food in someone's house.

Children's faith in the home and at school

Although the gurdwara is pivotal in the community, Sikh homes are just as much places of faith. From the child's point of view, home is the place where the faith is absorbed from older family members and by participating in what the adults do. Teachers debate whether spirituality is inborn or taught to children, but with Sikhs the presence of spirituality in everyone is so obvious that they don't feel the need to talk about it. Sikh children to whom I put the question, 'Do you know who God is?' looked at me with great surprise as if the question was too obvious for words – 'That's the person who created me and the Sikhs and the other people too,' said a 7-year-old boy. A 13-year-old, more reflective, said, 'God is the truth. He has made the world.' An 8-year-old girl explained to me, 'I know God loves me because I love other people.' Teachers can draw on this faith in the classroom, because pupils, especially at primary age, are actually willing to talk about what they believe, as long as the teacher has enough background knowledge to show that they recognise the words and concepts the child is talking about. If the teacher does not show recognition and familiarity with some of the home vocabulary, the pupil may feel that it is not even worth the effort to explain what they believe and do. As one 10-year-old girl commented, 'The RE that we're doing about, that's all my teacher wants to know. She doesn't know much ... It's like she don't know so she has to read it out of a book.'

Prayer too is something that Sikh children think is a matter of course. They are not all taught formal prayers from an early age, but they are taught to talk to God in their own words, and they sit with older relatives when they pray. The mother or granny will sit with a child in her lap while she does Naam jap (continuous recital of God's name), and as a result the child learns to do the same without even being aware of it. Look at even 4- or 5-year-old Sikh children in school when a tape of Naam jap is played – they will immediately start to join in. Children also listen to the shabads

(hymns from the Guru Granth Sahib) which are at the heart of Sikh community prayer and absorb these very gradually, often not fully understanding them. Children are encouraged to join in this kirtan singing, and many children have tabla or harmonium lessons and learn to accompany the hymn-singing from a very early age. Music is a part of Sikh prayer where the congregation can abandon themselves to the worship of God in a way which is completely beyond words, and even children experience this although they may not be able to articulate it. Don't be surprised or afraid if you play shabads in the classroom and a child shows some of this experience.

Sewa: to serve God's world

Prayer is one of the three basic principles of Sikhism expressed in a very common Sikh saying: 'Pray, earn an honest living and share what you have.' The second and third parts of this are clearly seen in the gurdwara in the communal voluntary work, the sharing of langar and the distribution of sweets to everyone at festivals. But this sense of service to others – called Sewa – extends much more widely than the gurdwara. The Sikh community is very generous. If you attend a procession on the occasion of Baisakhi or any festival, you will see all sorts of food shared with everyone who is out on the street. The Sikh community encourage their youngsters to be aware of the needs of the wider community, and there are enthusiastic partici-pants in activities like the charity bike rides, or the 'Khalsa Aid' to Kosovo where a group of young Sikhs took lorry loads of provisions to the Muslim refugees. Sikhs see the human race as one, and adapt their service according to the needs of the time. Perhaps because it is a young religion, Sikhism is able to adapt to the needs of the time and place where it finds itself. For example, children at activities in gurdwaras in England will often be given pizza or chips and beans as langar.

Sikhs like a challenge, and there are plenty facing Sikhs in this society. Everyone knows of the struggle to allow the wearing of the turban when the first immigrants came to England, but there are more subtle challenges still facing Sikhs. Many are vegetarian, and this is not always easy on social occasions. There is a sense of needing to protect the community's ideals in a society which is very materialistic. When the mother works outside the home, the old ways of passing on traditions are not so easy to keep up, and not every family now has a granny who was brought up in Punjab. It is a challenge to keep up the old practices at home, and parents have to make a big effort. With work pressure, even attending the gurdwara is not so easy. Then there is the question of language. Voluntary community organisations help to overcome some of these difficulties by opening Sunday schools or language and music classes. Gurdwaras and community centres provide forums for parents and young people to discuss the problems facing families: drugs, alcohol, mixed marriages, divorce and so on, the problems that challenge all communities in Britain today.

The challenge of teaching Sikhism

As teachers, especially teachers of RE (whether specialist or not), we have our own set of challenges. We should provide an ethos in the school community which allows pupils to feel confident and proud of whatever faith community they belong to. We should take care to emphasise the qualities that are common to us all. Collective worship themes, for example, should have topics accessible to all religions, but allowing for the special characteristics of a particular faith to be celebrated. Textbooks need to be chosen for their truthfulness to the living variety of faith communities. As teachers we need to have gone beyond the textbook before we start, and not only for our Sikh pupils but for all our pupils it is essential that we recognise that every faith has diverse expressions. No pupil should be made to feel less because their particular group does not conform to the norms of the dominant group in their religious faith – a Sikh with cut hair should not be made to feel less of a Sikh than a Sikh who keeps his long hair.

> Complete peace and harmony is satisfaction in your own life and self. Wars are caused by self-righteousness of people who are convinced they are right and everyone else's thinking is wrong, so they try to take over so EVERYONE can be just like them. If this happened, there would be no difference between people. People are different and no one should impose their opinions and way of life on others – this will lead to conflict.
>
> *Nishae, 15-year-old Sikh girl*

> It's very important for Sikhs to know Panjabi, the mother tongue of our culture and religion. The Guru Granth Sahib and all the other religious books of Sikhism are written in Panjabi. If we don't know Panjabi, we are depriving ourselves of access to the ocean of knowledge.
>
> *Virpal Kaur*

'For the destitute, Your Name is wealth. For the homeless, Your Name is home. For the lowly, Your Name is honour. You grant your gifts to every heart. Creator of all and cause of all causes You understand our deepest thoughts. You alone can grasp Your vastness. You are suffused in your own radiance. You alone can fully praise yourself. Says Nanak – no other can fathom You.

Sukhmani of Guru Arjan

How can an insignificant creature like myself Express the vastness and wonder of thy creation?

Guru Nanak: Jap Ji Sahib]

As RE teachers we have to do our homework carefully. The textbooks do not provide the full picture, so we need to go out into the community and find out for ourselves. As we look at faith practices, we need to avoid the trap of over-simplistic 'translations' of apparent similarities. For example, prasad is *not* like the Eucharist, a granthi is *not* a priest or imam, Amrit is *not* baptism. Training and professional development opportunities could be used to give staff the opportunity to learn and understand some of the religious language commonly used by pupils. They could also be used to share questions and have some of them answered by the RE inspector or by representatives of sections of the local community (always being aware of the existence of diverse views within the same faith).

In the classroom, religion should be approached as something which is already alive and a way of life for the pupils. They are already in many ways the experts, and all we need to do as teachers is approach their faith with knowledge, respect and understanding. We can stimulate discussion and sharing by using artefacts as a starting point. Again, knowledge is essential: we should know the etiquette for handling religious objects, and be aware of how the children see these used at home or in their place of worship. For Sikh pupils, the Five Ks are important whether or not they actually wear them themselves, and a teacher should use the right vocabulary to describe them. However, a Sikh pupil, while she can describe how her dad keeps a comb in his hair, may still ask the teacher 'why?' in the course of a class discussion. It is best to try and anticipate questions, but if you are unable to answer it is always better to say, 'I'll go and find out' than to make up an answer. Sometimes in discussion a pupil may use an expression that the teacher knows is inaccurate. For example, she may refer to a Guru as God. Rather than say, 'NO, he's a Guru', it is best to turn the statement so that it causes the child to reflect – 'Who is this in the picture? Is it really God? Can you see God?' Careful questioning can lead the pupil to clarify their own understanding of what they are saying.

What the pupils need

The key question a teacher needs to ask him- or herself about the teaching of RE applies not only to Sikhism but also to every religion: are we looking for spiritual development in the pupils or are we reinforcing external and ritualistic differences? But it is absolutely crucial in teaching about Sikhism as often much is made of external appearance both by some sections of the Sikh community and by all textbooks. What do pupils themselves want? In my experience what they want is to talk about and touch their own spiritual development. When the door is opened in real dialogue with pupils, both they and the teacher experience awe and wonder in its true sense.

Dhan Darshan

Ideas for teaching about the Sikhs for children aged 4–14

Major area of study	For 4–7-year-olds	For 7–11-year-olds	For 11–14-year-olds
Sikhism in the local area and the region **Living as a Sikh in Britain today**	• Learn that there are Sikh communities in our region, find out how many, where, and what their buildings are like; • Think and talk about why people might be proud to be Sikhs in Britain today, and why it might sometimes be a challenge to live a Sikh way of life; • *Make suggestions about the value and interest of having a Sikh community in our area.*	• Consider why many Sikh people now live in cities like London, Nottingham, Glasgow, Derby, Leicester and Birmingham; • Find out about one of your region's Sikh centres and gurdwaras: What is it like? What is its history? • Find out about how Sikhs in your area celebrate Vaisakhi or Guru Nanak's birthday; • *Develop their ideas about fairness and respect in the light of some examples of Sikh teaching: what might this mean for us? What might it mean for our town?*	• Learn more about the Sikh communities in the local area or the region; • Use census data and local directories to study the Sikh communities in the region; • *Consider what can be learned from Sikh human rights work or youth and education work, or a Sikh charity: how might these examples of Sewa challenge 'western' attitudes?* • *Consider whether and in what ways your own way of life might be influenced by your study of Sikhs.*
God **Sikh beliefs about God**	• Talk about some of the Sikh beliefs about God found in the Mool Mantar; • *Discuss their own thoughts and beliefs about God.*	• Find out why the Mool Mantar is a special prayer for Sikhs; • Explore how the Ik Onkar is used by Sikhs; • Discuss some Sikh beliefs about God identified in the Mool Mantar; • *Consider the words of a prayer, poem or piece of writing that they like or think is important;* • *Discuss the reasons why some people think that keeping God in mind at all times is really worthwhile;* • *Reflect on their own beliefs about God and compare them with the beliefs of other faiths studied.*	• Explore and explain the Sikh perceptions of God as described in the Mool Mantar; • Identify some Sikh beliefs about God which are similar to those found in other religions studied, and think about these similarities and any differences; • Explain what the revelation of God's message means to a Sikh; • *Consider how religious views are exemplified in life today;* • *Analyse how their own ideas about God compare with those of a Sikh.*
Authority **Sources of authority in Sikhism**	• Listen to stories from the life of Guru Nanak; • Find out why the Guru Granth Sahib is so called, and how it is treated by Sikhs; • *Reflect on the relevance today of some of Guru Nanak's teachings;* • *Consider why they consider some books to be special and how they treat things which are special;* • *Consider who has taught them something special.*	• Listen to stories about some gurus such as Guru Nanak, Guru Har Gobind and Guru Gobind Singh and discuss some of their teachings, characters and meanings: why have these stories lasted for hundreds of years? • Watch a video and discuss how the Guru Granth Sahib is treated and used in the gurdwara: what does this kind of respect show us about the Sikhs? • *Consider the greatest lesson about life they have ever been taught – what was it, how did they learn, and what difference does it make?* • *Reflect on what lessons about life they would like to pass on to younger children – or, one day, to their own children.*	• Explain how several of the Ten Gurus contributed to the Sikh view of life and beliefs; • What can be learnt about the Gurus from Sikh stories? What made them inspirational leaders? • What is the significance of the Guru Granth Sahib for Sikhs? What does it mean to treat the Guru Granth Sahib as a living Guru? • Read and comment on selected key passages from the Guru Granth Sahib; • *Consider a person they admire and comment on what that person taught them that is of real value;* • *Discuss the influences which affect their thinking and behaviour and consider how they decide which to follow and which to ignore.*

Major area of study	For 4–7-year-olds	For 7–11-year-olds	For 11–14-year-olds
Family and community life **Sikh family and community life**	• Find out why Sikhs do not cut their hair; • Discover the meanings of the Sikh names Kaur and Singh; • Watch a video of, or make a visit to, a gurdwara; • *Talk about the signs or symbols of belonging in their lives;* • *Talk about the importance of names and find out the meaning of their own names;* • *Reflect on their experience of a gurdwara and compare it to a special place they go to themselves.*	• Visit a gurdwara and discover its role in the Sikh community; • Listen to Sikh hymns and music; • Listen to a Sikh talking about their beliefs and how these influence behaviour and attitudes in Sikh daily life; • Discover why Amritsar is a special place for Sikhs; • *Reflect on their experiences and feelings during the visit to the Gurdwara;* • *Consider why worshipping together is important in many religions;* • *Consider the influences which affect the way they live their lives;* • *Talk about special places they like to visit.*	• Explain the role and the importance of the gurdwara to the Sikh community: what difference does the langar make to how Sikhs see themselves and the world? • Talk to a Sikh about the value of faith and worship in their lives – raise questions and suggest answers.; • Explore the significance of family life, the community of the gurdwara and the Five Ks for Sikhs; • Explore Sikh traditions which mark significant points in their lives and identify any historical or cultural links; • *Discuss the role faith and worship can play in people's lives;* • *Explain carefully how generosity is exemplified in the langar: do we need structures, rules and community agreements to make us more generous?* • *Talk to Sikh teenagers about their lives and compare them with their own;* • *Consider special times and symbols which mark momentous occasions in their lives.*
Beliefs and values **Sikh beliefs, values and attitudes;** **Celebrations and festivals**	• Talk about the Sikh belief that everyone is equal; • Discover how the birthday of Guru Nanak is celebrated; • Explore why Sikhs have a ceremony for naming a baby; • *Reflect on their own attitude and behaviour towards others in the light of the Sikh belief in equality;* • *Talk about how they like to celebrate their own birthdays;* • *Discuss the celebrations surrounding the birth of baby in their own family or community.*	• Discover why Sikhs believe all are equal before God; • Discover the origins of the festival of Baisakhi and how it is celebrated today; • Listen to a Sikh talking about the Amrit ceremony, the importance of the Khalsa and the significance of the Five Ks; • Discuss their own views on equality, making links to Sikh views; • *Consider the origins of some of the festivals they celebrate;* • *Talk about the benefits and drawbacks of 'belonging' to a family, community or organisation;* • *Talk about the important stages in life and how these are celebrated;* • *Reflect on how Sikh beliefs, values and attitudes could influence the lives of non-Sikhs.*	• Explain a Sikh's views on other religions, identifying historical links; • Explore Sikh values such as tolerance, equality, service to others and human rights; • Explore the tensions between abiding strictly to distinctive principles for living, and living in a secularised society; • *Consider their own attitudes and behaviour towards others who hold differing views;* • *Discuss and agree on a charter of principles by which to live and compare this with the charter on human rights;* • *Discuss the concept of 'Haumai' and consider the affect this may have on people's lives;* • *Consider the obligations and restrictions they have in their own lives and evaluate whether they are appropriate.*

Representing religions in RE
Into practice

In this final section, Lat Blaylock examines the challenges to the teacher of RE that the six preceding chapters offer, and urges an approach to RE that builds confidence upon understanding for any teacher. The insights of our teams of 'insiders' yield one kind of picture of good RE, which may clarify the professionalism of any RE practitioner.

In the preceding chapters of this book, teachers from within six faiths have tried to present the challenging, diverse, awkward and endlessly subtle contours of their religions, in ways that are alert to the difficult task of teaching RE in Britain today. As you have read these, perhaps you share my sense of both the significance and the difficulty of the task of RE. Our subject is significant because its contribution to education is (at its best) unique: global in scope, but more about the hearts and minds of the learners than anything else. RE has become the opposite of indoctrination – mind-opening, spiritual, free-thinking and yet also seeking to be true to many traditions, in touch with many histories and many stories of what it means to be human.

The issues and questions that our author teams have been considering include:

- **What are the religions?** The politics of representation is about defining and controlling the religious and the curricular. We have been trying to give some ownership of the religions in RE to those who believe and practise in each of six traditions, and are also 'classroom insiders' for RE. It has not been possible to expand the project to include members of other religious communities, and agnostics and atheists – who may also care about good RE. But it would have been desirable, because RE is about world views or life stances as well as about religions.

- **Who speaks for the religions in education?** Can any Christian speak of all Christianity, and any Hindu of all Hinduism? We know this is impossible. Our response to this has been to seek a balance of different kinds of Christians or Hindus in our writing teams, but we are well aware of the partial and provisional nature of the outcomes. Perhaps the only good defence against the distortion of a single perspective is alertness to the range of perspectives, even from within one faith, on what is the essence of the faith.

- **Can academic understandings help practice more?** How can academic explorations of the interrelationships between culture, identity and religion in contemporary society be brought into the service of RE teaching more effectively? We have high respect for the academic and independent analysis of religion in education, and Robert Jackson's introductory chapter shows some of the issues of representation which impact on RE's self-understanding. But in this modest piece of work, we have concentrated on the religious believers' perspectives. This picks up the idea of 'reflexivity' from Professor Jackson's introduction (see page 4).

- **Can teachers' confidence be increased?** A key need for teachers is to be sure that courses, textbooks, learning strategies and resources are fair, balanced, accurate and authentic, as well as engaging, interesting, relevant and challenging. Each of our writing groups has approached this problem differently. Some of the articles address themselves to 'dos and don'ts' quite explicitly, where others seek a more descriptive way of presenting the religion. In every case, it has been interesting and helpful to those involved in the writing to test their ideas with others. We hope

> Our subject is significant because its contribution to education is (at its best) unique: global in scope, but more about the hearts and minds of the learners than anything else.

this helpfulness is transmitted to you, the users of the book. Being confident goes with being tentative: authentic RE is not about complete accounts of religions, but does imply a depth to pupils' learning.

- **How can teachers reflect the diversity within each religion?** Providing for clear and straightforward learning in the 5–16 age-range is challenging enough, but each tradition is internally diverse too, as our articles show. Even the simple devices of saying 'Some Hindus…' or 'Many Buddhists…' when we speak of a faith in the classroom assist children to learn progressively that all religions include a wide variety of practice and understanding. As pupils grow older, understanding the main groups within a faith can become the explicit focus of study. Our writers have also been noticing that each tradition contains its traditionalists and progressives, and places its radicals in tension with its conservatives. If teachers, at least, remember that liberal Islam and fundamentalist Islam are currents in the same stream, then clarity about diversity is a possible learning outcome.

- **In what ways can school RE enable more authentic learning from religion?** In recent years, teachers seem to have become more confident about RE's potential to contribute to the 'personal search' of learners, or to provide for learning from religion. But this potentiality of the subject is still in need of building up. These articles suggest some ways of helping all children to get to grips with what they might learn from religions they do not believe, and will never follow themselves. A moment's reflection by any teacher of RE can usually identify things learned from the faiths we teach, but do not own. Such learning from religion deserves to be informed by the spiritual insights of the 'faith insiders' in this collection. Any RE pedagogy that neglected spirituality or edification or skills such as engagement, reflection and thoughtfulness in response would be inadequate. So our writers have, in each case, looked for ways to enable pupils to access the richness of their tradition's wisdom.

What do teachers need and want?

RE professionals want to be accurate, rounded, fully informed interpreters of the riches of religion to those who undervalue the spiritual, or are ill-informed.

In my advisory work, it is my privilege to meet over 2,000 teachers of RE each year. They are, in some ways, heroes of the global village. Among these people, the desire to move RE towards a more authentic encounter with religious communities 'as they are' is a strong motivation. Teachers of RE are ambitious to give young people authentic guidance to a complex field, to go on learning about the religious and the spiritual for themselves, to hear voices from inside a faith that understand what it's like inside a classroom, to be able to enliven education with examples beyond the merely factual, to help to identify and counter stereotypes, to picture faith positively in the future, without ever minimising the potentialities of religion's 'dark side'.

These ambitions are plastic: they are reshaped by the achievement of the subject every couple of years, and teachers of RE want more, better resources with which to do the job. The newly moulded ambitions of the RE teacher at the moment include listening to exactly the people who have so generously contributed to this book. RE professionals want to be accurate, rounded, fully informed interpreters of the riches of religion to those who undervalue the spiritual, or are ill-informed.

Seven tensions RE has to live with

In RE, the progress in quality of the subject over recent years has been tense: it feels as if there are many points of tension which those who teach the subject have to try and hold together. In this particular volume, we have been keenly aware of seven of these in our work together. They are worth sharing because they are the tensions a teacher must live with too.

- **The religion is one, but not all the same.** Some of our teams of authors have reflected on the article that they have written together by saying, 'I could not

have done this alone, because my experience in the religion is too narrow and particular'. In RE, where learning that sentences that start 'All Hindus…' or 'All Christians…' are mostly false, teachers begin by teaching what is distinctive to the religion studied, but often need to move on to see how different two Muslims or two Buddhists might be from each other.

- **History, origins and foundations matter, but contemporary lived experience may build the bridge of relevance to the pupil better.** Every teacher, approaching a religion for the first time with a class, needs to determine where to begin. The starting points often suggested by the legitimate concerns of the faith community may be for accuracy, authenticity, depth, conceptual or belief-focused understanding and comprehensiveness. But these can only come alive for pupils if the concerns of teachers (for interest, relevance, a good 'hook' to begin the lesson) are also layered into the design of the curriculum. This persistent tension raises a question that deserves the careful analysis of every teacher: how can our RE play fairly with the concerns of the faith and the needs of the class?

- **Distinctiveness and uniqueness are in tension with interreligious dialogue and common humanity.** Several of our contributors have wanted to say, in various ways, that the blurring of distinctions between religions by those who look upon them from distant secular perspectives is an offence to good education. Yet others want to say that it is from within their Christian, Muslim or Jewish traditions that the impulse to 'one world' arises. The tension this illustrates is profound: is it our common humanity or our differences that we must most attend to? In general terms, this book takes the view that religions taught authentically, with regard to their own characteristic passions and distinctiveness, come first in RE, but attending to the ways religions interact, positively and negatively, is an essential second step. Teachers may want today to move their practice in the direction of emphasising what is unique about a religion, or in the direction of exploring commonalities, but none of us will dispense with the need to rebalance this tension many times.

- **100% accuracy is the standard, but teachers have many, many priorities.** We have been very aware of the pressures teachers live with as we have made this book. Editorial decisions have often been driven by the question 'but will the primary class teacher make sense of this?' Sometimes we've included material that many teachers with other specialisms doing a bit of RE will find a stretch. But it is worth saying clearly that when we teach a religion to which we don't belong, settling for less than 100% accuracy is a dereliction of professionalism. The solutions to inaccurate teaching are not easy: training, subject specialism and professionalism are central, and individual teachers doing their best are not to blame for the difficulties created by the shortage of specialist RE teachers. Having said that, we think that 100% accuracy is a tough standard, but it isn't negotiable.

- **Professional confidence is essential for good teaching, but misplaced confidence leads to misrepresentation.** It is possible to imagine poor RE teaching that is unencumbered by an awareness of its own ignorance! We aim to support, rather than undermine professional confidence in these pages. If you read one of the articles, and feel less confident in your RE work, then we trust that you will be able to find some helpful professional development from a SACRE, a professional RE book, a PCfRE project or another source. But many will read a section of the book on a particular religion and be encouraged: the papers clarify good practice and raise thoughtful and provocative questions about the way we present each religion.

- **So much to say, so little opportunity.** RE is a tiny slice of the curricular pie – maybe an hour a week is more time than the subject gets on average. And in a secularising society like the UK today, most learners don't come with much 'prior learning' about religion, just maybe a bag of prejudices. So how to make that hour

Teachers may want today to move their practice in the direction of emphasising what is unique about a religion, or in the direction of exploring commonalities, but none of us will dispense with the need to rebalance this tension many times.

count? The writers in this volume have taken the view that RE should be ambitious about what can be achieved, should seek a global picture, historically textured and personally focused, of each religion. Doing less, but doing it well is perhaps the guidance that is worth emphasising here. The tool of careful curriculum selection, well informed by religious 'insiders' is worth applying thoughtfully, so that we don't seek to show children 'everything about Sikhism' in RE – but what we do show them should be authentic, potentially profound, and connected to their own questions and concerns. That is perhaps the 'tensest tension' of all.

- **The ambitiousness of this project is in tension with its modesty.** It's ridiculous, in a way, that a small group of teachers from many religions should hope to move RE through this short book: here we come with our articles and insights, aiming to improve RE's representation of all the vastness and depth of world religions, in the face of indifference and some hostility from millions of pupils and even from many teachers too. But acknowledging the complexity and difficulty of the field, we still hope that teachers will welcome the complex, subtle and strongly held views they find in these pages.

Good RE is suitably modest: we can't transform the understanding of religion in the UK swiftly or simply, but we can make a difference by opening windows into faith from classrooms in ways that seek integrity.

What is good RE like?

Generalisations from the six articles from faith in this book provide a clear picture of some characteristics of good RE. We have sought to model these principles in each of the articles.

- Good RE engages with aspects of the whole of a religious tradition, but is clear about the standpoint of the writer(s) within the tradition.

- Good RE is at least as alert to the contemporary in a religion as to the historical – questions of founders and leaders matter, but so do questions about the relevance of the materials to learners today.

- Good RE is open to what is positive about each religion: highlighting what treasures adherents find in their faith, and also what the religion offers to any learner (negatives matter as well, but are often already present in stereotypical views of the Islamic, the Christian or the Hindu).

- Good RE is not representative, never claims to have finished the study of a religion, and owns up happily to being partial and tentative. But good RE is also authentic: those patches of a religion that can be examined are approached in depth, both critically and empathetically.

- Good RE must be accessible through ordinary teachers with no particular background but with a commitment to doing RE better. When considering accuracy and realism, we have found it helpful to ask: 'Would this happen in science? In Maths?' If teams of teachers are asked to deal with many religions, a baseline of the opportunity to access accurate and authentic resources and to develop a professionalism about RE is necessary. Good RE does not exist without the careful planning and development of some teacher-expertise.

- Good RE is willing to be personal at appropriate points, noticing that in one sense there is no such thing as Buddhism, just a lot of people who are Buddhists. Many RE teachers have become very skilled at being personal, allowing emotion, faith and passion to play a part in learning while avoiding coercion.

- Good RE is suitably modest: we can't transform the understanding of religion in the UK swiftly or simply, but we can make a difference by opening windows into faith from classrooms in ways that seek integrity.

List of contributors

Adiccabandhu is a primary teacher of RE and a member of the Clear Vision Trust (Western Buddhist Order). He is a Buddhist.

Liz Andrews is a primary teacher with experience in Scotland and England. She is a Buddhist, a member of the Clear Vision Trust (Western Buddhist Order).

Gary Beesley is a secondary RE teacher in Cumbria. He is a Buddhist in the Tibetan tradition.

Lat Blaylock is the Executive Officer of the Professional Council for RE and used to teach RE in Leicester. He is a Christian.

Sarah Edwards is a secondary RE teacher in Birmingham. She is a Christian with links to Baptist and Mennonite traditions.

Sundeep Gill is a primary school teacher of RE in Middlesex. She is a Sikh.

Robert Jackson is Professor of Religion and Education at the University of Warwick's Religion and Education Research Unit. He is the Editor of the British Journal of Religious Education.

Anne Marie Jones is a primary RE co-ordinator at an Anglican school in Cheshire. She is a Christian in the Church of England.

Paul Kassapian is an RE subject leader with responsibility for spiritual development and liturgy at a Catholic comprehensive school in Hertfordshire. He is a Christian in the Roman Catholic tradition.

Fatima Khan is a secondary school RE teacher in Birmingham. She is a Muslim.

Anne Krisman is a specialist RE teacher in special education – she works at a special school in the London Borough of Redbridge. She is Jewish.

Harvey Kurzfield taught RE in Cornwall until his recent retirement. He is Jewish.

Jay Lakhani provides Hindu education to many schools and students, from the Vivekananda Centre in Neasden, London. He is a Hindu.

Surinder Lall is an RE subject leader at a school in London, and a Farmington Fellow. She is a Sikh.

Imran Mogra is subject leader for RE at a Birmingham LEA primary school with a large majority of Muslim pupils. He is a Muslim.

Naina Parmar is an RE subject leader in a primary school in North London. She is a Hindu.

Andy Thelwell is an RE teacher at a boys' comprehensive school in Hertfordshire. He is a Christian, loosely within the Methodist tradition.

Carol Tibbs has recently retired from her job as an RE teacher at a secondary school in Tower Hamlets. She has been a Hindu for more than two decades.

Sandra Vincent is the head teacher of a primary school in Essex. She is Jewish.

Neera Vyas is a secondary teacher of RE in Wrexham, Wales. She is a Hindu.

Marianne Heathcote Woodbridge is an RE adviser with RE Today Services, and used to be a primary RE subject leader. She is a Christian.

PCFRE is pleased to thank all those who have given generously of their time, experience and insight in creating this book.

Bibliography and resources

Publications from RE Today Services

Ring 0121 472 4242 to order or for a catalogue, or buy online at www.retoday.org.uk

The Professional Council for RE provides some free resources from back issues of our journal *Resource* on the web at www.pcfre.org.uk.

Teaching RE **5–11 and 11–16**: 32-page volumes of teachers' ideas and classroom activities on each of the six world religions addressed in this book.

Pictorial Guides: Six simple booklets each containing thirty or more copiable black-and-white line drawings, and an introductory text for teachers on each of the six religions.

Many other resources for teaching RE are available from RE Today Services.

Religions in the UK Directory, edited by Paul Weller (Inter Faith Network, University of Derby, 2001. ISBN: 0-901437-96-4)

The **Shap Working Party on World Religions in Education** publishes an excellent annual journal with its calendar of religious festivals. PO Box 38580, London SW1P 3XF, e-mail shap@natsoc.c-of-e.org.uk

Artefact suppliers

Articles of Faith
Resource House
Kay Street
Bury BL9 6BU
Tel: 0161 763 6232
Fax: 0161 763 5366

Religion in Evidence
TTS
Nun Brook Road
Hathwaite
Sutton-in-Ashfield
Nottinghamshire NG17 2H9
Tel: 0800 318 686
Fax: 0800 137 525

Artefacts to Order
17 South Brink
Wisbech
Cambridgeshire PE13 1JQ
01945 587 452

A few faith community suppliers

Your local **Christian bookshops** will be a good place to start with Christian artefacts.

DTF *(Asian, especially Sikh, books and artefacts)*
117 Soho Road
Handsworth
Birmingham B21 9ST

ISKCON Educational Services
(Hindu resources and artefacts)
Bhaktivedanta Manor
Hilfield Lane
Aldenham
Watford
Herts WD2 8EZ
Tel/ Fax: 01923 859 578

Throssel Hole Buddhist Bookshop *(and artefacts)*
Carrshield
Near Hexham
Northumberland NE47 8AL
Tel: 01434 345 204
Fax: 01434 345 216

IQRA Trust *(Islamic)*
24 Culross Street
London W1Y 3HE
Tel: 0207 491 1572
Fax: 0207 493 7899

Manor House *(Jewish)*
80 East End Road
Finchley
London N3 2SY
Tel: 0181 349 9484
Fax: 0181 346 7430